# THE GOSPEL OF JOHN

WILLIAM MACDONALD

*Developed as a study course by Emmaus Correspondence School, founded in 1942.*

Published by:

Emmaus Correspondence School
(A division of ECS Ministries)
PO Box 1028
Dubuque, IA 52004-1028
(563) 585-2070
www.ecsministries.org

Revised 2006 (AK '06)
Reprinted 2008 (AK '06)

ISBN 978-0-940293-27-4



Cover by Ragont Design, Barrington, IL



*Printed in the United States of America*

# Student Instructions

John the apostle was an old man when he wrote his Gospel. It was written years after the other three "memoirs" of Christ had been put into circulation. Already the Church was being plagued by error and attacks upon the Person and work of God's beloved Son. So John wrote the last word on the sojourn in this scene of heaven's Beloved. His purpose is to say to men, "Behold your God."

As you study the story of Jesus, as unfolded in this Gospel, we trust the Holy Spirit will guide you until you fling yourself at Jesus' feet with Thomas of old and say, "My Lord and my God!"

## Lessons You Will Study

## Course Components

This course has two parts: this study course and a separate exam booklet.

## How to Study

This study has twelve chapters that will greatly help you. Each chapter has its own exam. Begin by asking God to open your heart to receive the truths He would teach you from His Word. Read the chapter through at least twice, once to get a general idea of its contents and then again, slowly, looking up all the Scripture references.

Begin studying immediately, or if you are in a group, as soon as the group begins. We suggest that you keep a regular schedule by trying to completing one chapter per week.

## Exams

In the exam booklet there is one exam for each chapter (Exam 1 covers chapter 1 of the course). Do not answer the questions by what you think or have always believed. The questions are designed to find out if you understand the material and the Scripture verses given in the course.

After you have completed each chapter, review the related exam, and see how well you know the answers. If you find that you are having difficulty answering the questions, review the material until you think you can answer the questions.

## How Your Exams are Graded

Your instructor will mark any incorrectly answered questions. You will be referred back to the place in the Bible or textbook where the correct answer is to be found. After finishing this course with a passing average, you will be awarded a certificate.

If you enrolled in a class, submit your exam papers to the leader or secretary of the class who will send them for the entire group to the Correspondence School.

See the back of the Exam Booklet for more information on returning the exams for grading.

CHAPTER

# 1

# The Gospel and How It Begins (John 1:1-18)

## Introduction to the Gospel

John's purpose in writing was that his readers might know that "Jesus is the Christ, the Son of God, and that believing, [they] might have life through His name" (20:31).

There are seven public miracles, or signs, in this Gospel, each designed to show to men that Jesus is God—(1) Turning of the water into wine at the wedding in Cana of Galilee (2:9). (2) Healing of the nobleman's son (4:46-54). (3) Healing of the crippled man at the pool of Bethesda (5:2-9).

(4) Feeding of the five thousand (6:1-14). (5) Jesus' walking on the Sea of Galilee to rescue the disciples from the storm (6:16-21). (6) Healing of the man who was blind from birth (9:1-7). (7) Raising of Lazarus from the dead (11:1-44). In addition to these seven performed in public, there is an eighth sign-miracle performed only for His disciples after the resurrection: the miraculous catch of fish (21:1-14).

Charles R. Erdman says of this Gospel, "It has induced more persons to follow Christ, it has inspired more believers to loyal service, it has presented to scholars more difficult problems, than any other book that could be named."

The *authorship* of this Gospel has been greatly debated in the past 150 years. This is undoubtedly because it gives such clear testimony to the deity of Jesus Christ. The attack has sought to prove the Gospel was not the work of an eye-witness but the work of an unknown genius who lived 50 to 100 years later. Thus it is supposed to reflect the thinking of the church about Christ and not what He Himself actually was, said, or did.

The Gospel itself is anonymous as to authorship, but there are many good reasons for believing that it was written by John the Apostle, one of the twelve. For example, the author was a Jew—the style of writing, the vocabulary, the familiarity with Jewish customs and characteristics, and the background of the Old Testament reflected in this Gospel all speak strongly of this. He was a Jew who lived in Palestine (1:28; 2:1, 11; 4:46; 11:18, 54; 21:1, 2). He knew Jerusalem and the temple intimately (5:2; 9:7; 18:1; 19:13, 17, 20, 41; also see 2:14-16; 8:20; 10:22). He was an eye-witness of what he narrates. There are many, many details of places, persons, time, manner (4:46; 5:14; 6:59; 12:21; 13:1; 14:5, 8; 18:6; 19:31). He was an apostle and shows intimate knowledge of the inner circle of the disciples and of the Lord Himself (6:19, 60, 61; 12:16; 13:22, 28; 16:19). Since the author is precise in naming the other disciples and does not name himself, it is presumed that the unnamed person of 13:23; 19:26; 20:2; 21:7, 20, is the Apostle John. Three important passages for further consideration of the eye-witness character of the author are 1:14; 19:35; and 21:24.

The *chronology* of our Lord's earthly ministry is gained from this Gospel. From the other three Gospels, the ministry of Christ would appear to have lasted only one year. The references to the annual feasts in John give us the duration of approximately three years for His public ministry. Note these references: The first feast of Passover (2:12, 13); "a feast" (5:1), possibly the Passover of Purim; second (or third) feast of Passover (6:4); the feast of Tabernacles (7:2); the feast of Dedication (10:22); and the last feast of Passover (12:1).

John is also precise in his references to time. While the other three writers are generally content with approximate references such as the third or ninth hours, John mentions the seventh hour (4:52), the third day (2:1), two days (11:6), and six days (12:1).

The *style and vocabulary* of this Gospel are unique except for the Epistles of John. The sentences are short and simple. They are Hebrew in thought although Greek in language. Usually the shorter the sentence the weightier the truth. The vocabulary is the most limited of all the Gospels but the most profound in meaning. Note these important words and the number of their occurrences: Father (118), believe (100), world (78), love (45), life (37), witness, bear record, etc. (47), light (24), etc.

One marked feature of this Gospel is the occurrence of the number seven and its multiples. The ideas of perfection and completion attach to this number throughout Scripture (see Genesis 2:1-3). In this Gospel the Spirit of God perfects and completes the revelation of God in the Person of Jesus Christ, so patterns based on the number seven are frequent.

The seven "I ams" of the Gospel are familiar. These are "The Bread of Life" (6:35, 41, 48, 51); "The Light of the World" (8:12; 9:5); "The Door" (10:7, 9); "The Good Shepherd" (10:11, 14); "The Resurrection and the Life" (11:25); "The Way, the Truth, and the Life" (14:6); and "The Vine" (15:1, 5). Not so familiar are the seven occurrences of "I am" without a predicate, that is, the simple statement. These are found in 4:26; 6:20; 8:24, 28, 58; 13:19; 18:5, 8. The last one is a double one.

In the sixth chapter which has to do with the Bread of Life, the Greek word for bread occurs 21 times, a multiple of seven. Part of the time it is rendered "loaves" and part of the time "bread." Also in the Bread of Life Discourse the expression "bread out of heaven" occurs just seven times and a similar expression "cometh down from heaven" occurs just seven times.

## The Prologue (1:1-18)

John begins his Gospel by speaking about *the Word*—but he does not explain at first who or what the Word is. A word is a unit of speech by which we express ourselves to others. But John is not speaking about a unit of speech but rather about a Person. That Person is the Lord Jesus Christ, the Son of God. John speaks of Him as the Word because God has fully expressed Himself to mankind in the Person of the Lord Jesus. By coming into the world, Christ has revealed to us what God is like and by dying for us on the Cross of Calvary, He has told us how much God loves us. Thus Christ is God's living Word to man, the expression of God's thoughts.

### 1. The Lord Jesus Introduced as the Word (1:1-5)

John starts in verse 1 with a statement that the Lord existed from all eternity. As far as the human mind can go back, the Lord Jesus was there. He never was created. He had no beginning. "The Word was with God." He had a separate and distinct personality. He was a real Person who lived with God. He not only dwelt with God, but He Himself was God. The Bible teaches that there is one God and that there are three Persons in the Godhead—the Father, the Son, and the Holy Spirit. All three of these Persons are God. In this verse, two of the Persons of the Godhead are mentioned—God the Father and God the Son. It is the first of many clear statements in this Gospel that *Jesus Christ is God.* It is not enough to say that He is a god, that He is godlike, or that He is divine. The Bible teaches that He *is* God.

Verse 2 would appear to be a repetition of what has been said, but actually it is not so. This verse teaches that Christ's personality and deity were without beginning. He did not become a Person for the first time as the Babe of Bethlehem. Nor did He somehow become a god after His resurrection, as some teach today. He is God from all eternity.

He Himself was not a created being; rather He was the Creator of all things—mankind, the animals, the heavenly planets, the angels—all things visible and invisible. If a thing was made, He made it. As Creator, He is, of course, superior to anything He has created. Actually all three Persons of the Godhead were involved in the work of creation: "God created the heaven and the earth" (Genesis 1:1). "The Spirit of God moved upon the face of the waters" (Genesis 1:2). "All things were created by him [Christ], and for him" (Colossians l:16b).

He was and is the source of life. The word here in verse 4 includes both physical and spiritual life. When we were born, we received physical life. When we are born again, we receive spiritual life. Both come from Him. The same One who supplied us with life is also the light of men. He provides the guidance and direction necessary for man. It is one thing to exist, but another thing to know how to live, to know the true purpose of life, and to know the way to heaven. The same One who gave us life is the One who provides us with light for the pathway we travel.

There are seven wonderful titles of our Lord Jesus Christ found in this opening chapter of the Gospel. He is called the Word (vv. 1, 14); the Light (vv. 5, 7); the Lamb of God (vv. 29, 36); the Son of God (vv. 34, 49); the Christ (Messiah) (v. 41); the King of Israel (v. 49); the Son of Man (v. 51). The first four titles, each of which is mentioned at least twice, seem to be universal in application. The last three titles, each of which is mentioned only once, had their first application to Israel, God's ancient people.

The entrance of sin brought darkness to the minds of men (1:5). It plunged the world into darkness in the sense that men in general neither knew God nor wanted to know Him. Into this darkness the Lord Jesus came—a light shining in a dark place. "The darkness comprehended it not," we read. This may mean that the darkness did not understand the Lord Jesus when He came into the world. Men did not realize who He really was, or why He had come. Another meaning, however, is given in the margin of the American Standard Version. ". . . the darkness overcame it not." Here the thought would be that man's rejection and enmity did not prevent the true light from shining.

## 2. The Ministry of John the Baptist (1:6-8)

These verses refer to John the Baptist who was sent by God as a forerunner of the Lord Jesus. His mission was to announce the coming of Christ and to tell the people to get ready to receive Him. He came to testify to the fact that Jesus was truly the Light of the world, so that all men might put their trust in Him. He did not attract attention to himself for then he would have been unfaithful to his appointed task. He pointed men to Jesus and not to himself.

## 3. The Coming of Christ into the World (1:9-18)

Other persons down through the ages have claimed to be guides and saviors, but the One to whom John witnessed was the genuine Light, the best and the truest Light (1:9). Another translation of this verse is, "The true Light, which, coming into the world, lightens every man." In other words, the expression "coming into the world" described *the true Light* rather than *every man.* It was by the coming of the true Light into the world that every man was lightened. This does not mean that every man has received some inward knowledge concerning Christ. Neither does it mean that all men have heard about the Lord Jesus at one time or another. Rather, it means that the Light shines upon all men, without regard to their nationality, race, or color. It also means that by shining on all men, the Lord Jesus has revealed men in their true character. By His coming into the world as the perfect Man, He has shown how imperfect all other men are. When a room is in darkness, you do not see the dust on the furniture. But when the light goes on, the room is seen as it actually is. In that same sense, the shining of the true Light reveals man as he actually is.

From the time of His birth in Bethlehem until the day He went back to heaven, He was in this very same world in which we now live (1:10). Indeed, He had more right to be here than anyone else. He had brought the whole world into being and was its rightful Owner. Instead of recognizing Him as the Creator, men thought that He was just another man like themselves. They treated Him like a stranger and an outcast.

"He came unto his own [things]," we read in verse 11. He was not trespassing on someone else's property. Rather, He was living on a planet which He himself had made. Moreover "His own [people] received him not." In a general sense, this might refer to all mankind, and it is true that almost all mankind rejected Him. But in a special sense, the Jewish nation was His chosen, earthly people. When He came into the world, He presented

Himself to the Jews as their Messiah, but they would not receive Him. So now He offers Himself to all mankind again and to those who receive Him, He gives the right or authority to become children of God (1:12). This verse tells us clearly how we can become children of God. It is not by good works, not by church membership, not by doing one's best—but by receiving Him, by believing on His Name.

To become a child in a physical sense, one must be born. So, also, to become a child of God, one must have a second birth. This is known as the new birth or conversion or being saved. Verse 13 tells us three ways by which the new birth does not take place, and the one way by which it does. It is "not of blood." This means that a person does not become a Christian through having Christian parents. Salvation is not passed down from parent to child through the blood stream. It is not "of the will of the flesh." In other words, a person does not have the power in his own flesh to produce the new birth. Although he must be willing in order to be saved, yet his own will is not enough to save him. It is not "of the will of man." No other man can save a person. A preacher, for instance, may be very anxious to see a certain person born again, but he does not have the power to produce this marvelous birth. How, then, does this birth take place? The answer is found in the words "but of God." This means simply that the power to produce the new birth does not rest with anything or anyone but God.

The "Word was made flesh" when Jesus was born as a Babe in the manger at Bethlehem (1:14). He had always existed as the Son of God with the Father in heaven, but He now chose to come into the world in a human body. The New King James Version is accurate in translating this expression, "the Word *became* flesh." He was never made or created; He Himself was the Creator of all things. But He became flesh in the sense that He came into the world as a Man.

He "dwelt among us," we read. It was not just a short appearance, about which there might be some mistake or misunderstanding. God actually came to this earth and lived here as a Man among men. The word "dwelt" means "tabernacled" or "pitched His tent." His body was the tent in which He dwelt among men for thirty-three years.

"And we beheld His glory," says John. In the Bible "glory" often means the bright, shining light which was seen when God was present. It also means the perfection and excellence of God. When the Lord Jesus was here on earth, He veiled His glory in a body of flesh. But there were two ways in which His glory became manifest. First, there was His moral glory. By this, we mean the radiance of His perfect life and character. There was no flaw or blemish in Him. He was perfect in all His ways. Every virtue was manifested in His life in exquisite balance. Then there was the visible outshining of His glory which took place on the Mount of Transfiguration (Matthew 17:1-2). The glory which the disciples saw indicated to them that He was truly the Son of God. Jesus is "the only begotten of the Father," that is, Christ is God's unique Son. God did not have any other Son like Him. In one sense, all true believers are sons of God. But Jesus is the Son of God—in a class all by Himself. As the Son of God, He is equal with God.

He is "full of grace and truth." He was full of undeserved kindness for others. But He was also completely honest and upright, and He never excused sin or approved evil. To be completely gracious and at the same time completely righteous is something that only God can be.

We read in verse 15 that John the Baptist testified that Jesus was the Son of God. Before the Lord entered upon His public ministry, John had been telling men about Him. When Jesus did arrive upon the scene, John said, in effect, "This is the One I have been describing to you." Jesus came *after John* so far as His birth and ministry were concerned. He was born six months after John and presented Himself to the people of Israel some time after John had been preaching and baptizing. But Jesus was "preferred before" John. He was greater than John; He was worthy of more honor, the simple reason being that He was before John. He existed from all eternity—the Son of God.

All who believe on the Lord Jesus receive spiritual strength out of His fullness (1:16). His fullness is so great that He can provide for all Christians in all countries and in all ages. The expression "grace for grace" probably means "grace upon grace" or "abundant grace." Here "grace" means God's gracious favor which He showers upon His beloved children.

In verse 17 John contrasts the Old Testament period and the New Testament era. The law given by Moses was not a display of grace. It commanded men to obey and condemned them to death if they failed to do so. It told men what was right but did not give them the power to do it. It was given to show men that they were sinners, but it could not save them from their sins. "But grace and truth came by Jesus Christ." He did not come to judge the world but to save those who were unworthy, who could not save themselves, and who were His enemies. That is grace—heaven's best for earth's worst.

Not only did grace come by Jesus Christ, but truth came by Him as well. He said of Himself, "I am . . . the truth." He was absolutely honest and faithful in all His words and works. He did not show grace at the expense of truth. Although He loved sinners, He did not love their sins.

"No man has seen God at any time," says John in verse 18. God is spirit and therefore is invisible. He does not have a human body. Although He did appear to men in the Old Testament in visible form as an Angel or as a Man, these appearances did not reveal what God is really like. They were merely temporary appearances by which He chose to speak to His people. The Lord Jesus is God's only begotten Son; He is God's unique Son; there is no other Son like Him. He ever occupies a place of special nearness to God the Father. Even when He was here on earth, Jesus was still in the bosom of the Father. He was one with God and equal with God. He has fully revealed to men what God is like. When men saw Jesus, they saw God. They heard God speak. They felt God's love and tenderness. God's thoughts and attitudes toward mankind have been fully told out by Christ.

CHAPTER

# 2

# First Impressions (John 1:19–3:36)

## The Testimony of John the Baptist (1:19-34)

When news reached Jerusalem that a man named John was telling the nation to repent because the Messiah was coming, the Jews sent a committee of priests and Levites to find out who this man was. The priests were those who carried on the important services in the temple, while the Levites were servants who attended to common duties there. "Who are you?" they asked. "Are you the long-awaited Messiah?"

Other men might have seized this opportunity for fame by claiming to be the Christ. But John was a faithful witness. His testimony was that he was not the Christ, that is, the Messiah (1:20). The Jews expected Elijah to return to the earth prior to the coming of Christ (Malachi 4:5). So they reasoned that if John was not the Messiah, then perhaps he was Elijah. But John assured them that he was not (1:21). In Deuteronomy 18:15, Moses had said, "The LORD your God will raise up for you a prophet like me from among you, from your brothers—it is to him you shall listen." The Jews remembered this prediction and thought that John might be the prophet mentioned by Moses. But again John said that it was not so.

The delegation would have been embarrassed to go back to Jerusalem without a definite answer, and so they asked John for a statement as to who he was. He responded in verse 23, "I am the voice of one crying in the wilderness," quoting from Isaiah 40:3. In other words, John stated that he was the predicted forerunner. He was the voice, and Israel was the wilderness. The people had become dry and barren, like a desert. John spoke of himself simply as a voice—a voice not to be seen, but only to be heard. John was the voice but Christ was the Word. The word needs a voice to make it known and the voice is of no value without a word. The Word is infinitely greater than the voice. It is our privilege, too, to be a voice for Him.

John's message was, "Make straight the way of the Lord." In other words, "The Messiah is coming. Remove everything in your life that would hinder you from receiving Him. Repent of your sins, so that He can come and reign over you as the King of Israel."

The Pharisees who made up the delegation were a strict sect of the Jews who prided themselves on their superior knowledge of the law and on their efforts to carry out the most minute details of the instructions of the Old Testament. Actually, many of them were hypocrites who tried to appear religious but who lived very sinful lives. They wanted to know what authority John had for baptizing if he was not one of the important persons whom they named (1:25).

"I baptize with water," said John in verse 26. He did not want anyone to think that *he* was important. His task was simply to prepare men for Christ. Whenever his hearers repented of their sins, he baptized them in water as an outward symbol of their inward change. "Among you stands one you do not know," continued John, referring of course to Jesus. The Pharisees did not recognize Him as the long looked-for Messiah. "Do not think of me as a great man," said John in effect. "The One you should be paying attention to is the Lord Jesus; yet you do not know who He really is." He is the One who is worthy! He came after John the Baptist, yet He deserves all the praise and the pre-eminence (1:27). It was the duty of a slave or a servant to untie his master's sandals. But John did not consider himself worthy to perform such a humble, lowly service for Christ. The exact location of Bethany (1:28) where John was ministering is not known. But we do know that it was on the east side of the Jordan River.

On the day following the visit of the Pharisees from Jerusalem, John looked up and saw Jesus approaching him (1:29). In the thrill and excitement of that moment, he cried out, "Behold! the Lamb of God, who takes away the sin of the world!" The lamb was a sacrificial animal among the Jews. God had taught them to slay a lamb and to sprinkle its blood as a sacrifice. The lamb was killed as a substitute and its blood shed so that sins might be forgiven. However, the blood of the lambs that were slain during the Old Testament period did not really put away sin. Those lambs were pictures or types, pointing forward to the fact that God would one day provide a Lamb who would actually bear away sin. All down through the years, godly Jews had waited for the coming of this Lamb. Now at last the time had come, and John the Baptist triumphantly announced the arrival of the true Lamb of God.

When he said that Jesus bears the sin of the world, he did not mean that everyone's sins are therefore forgiven. The death of the Lord Jesus was great enough in value to pay for the sins of the whole world, but only those sinners who receive Him as Lord and Savior are forgiven.

John never grew weary of reminding men that he was only preparing the way for Someone greater than himself who was coming (1:30). Jesus was greater than John to the same extent that God is greater than man. John was born a few months before Jesus, but Jesus had existed from all eternity. When John said in verse 31, "I myself did not know him," he did not necessarily mean that he had never seen Him before. It is probable that John and Jesus were well acquainted since they were cousins. But John had not recognized his cousin as being the Messiah and did not do so until the time of His baptism. John's mission was to prepare the way of the Lord, and then to point Him out to the people of Israel when He appeared. It was for this reason that John baptized people in water—to prepare them for the coming of Christ. It was not for the purpose of attracting disciples to himself.

The reference in verse 32 was to the time when John baptized the Lord Jesus in the Jordan River. After the Lord went up out of the water, the Spirit of God descended like a dove and rested on Him (Matthew 3:16). God had revealed to John that the Messiah was coming and that when He came, the Spirit of God would descend upon Him and stay on Him. Therefore, when this happened to Jesus, John realized that this was the One who would baptize with the Holy Ghost (1:33).

The Holy Ghost is the Holy Spirit, a Person, one of the three Persons in the Godhead. He is equal with God the Father and God the Son. John baptized with water but Jesus would baptize with the Holy Spirit. The baptism with the Holy Ghost took place on the day of Pentecost (Acts 1:5 and Acts 2:4, 38) when the Holy Spirit came down to dwell in the body of every believer and to make each believer a member of the Church, the body of Christ (1 Corinthians 12:13).

John now bore positive witness to the fact that Jesus of Nazareth was the Son of God who was foretold as coming into the world (1:34). When John said that Christ was the Son of God, he meant that He was God the Son.

## Andrew, John, and Peter Become Disciples (1:35-42)

The day mentioned here in verse 35 is the third day that has been mentioned. John was with two of his own disciples. These men had heard John preach and believed what he said. But as yet they had not met the Lord Jesus. Now John again bore public witness to the Lord. On the previous day, he had spoken of His Person (the Lamb of God) and His work (which takes away the sin of the world). Now he simply drew attention to His Person. Notice that his message was short, simple, selfless, and all about the Savior (1:37). And by his faithful preaching, John lost two disciples, but he was glad to see them following Jesus.

The Savior is always interested in those who follow Him (1:38). Here He showed His interest by turning to the two disciples and asking them a question. He knew the answer to the question; He knows all things. But He wanted them to express their desire in words. Their answer showed they wanted to be with the Lord and to get to know Him better. They were not satisfied merely to meet Him. They longed to have fellowship with Him. They called Him "Rabbi," the Hebrew word for master or teacher.

No one with a genuine desire to learn more of the Savior is ever turned away. Jesus invited the two to the place where He was staying at that time—probably a very poor dwelling, compared to modern homes. They spent that night in the same home as the Creator of the universe. They were among the very first members of the Jewish nation to recognize the Messiah.

The Lord's invitation was extended to them about "the tenth hour" (i.e., 4 o' clock in the afternoon). It would be interesting to know how late they stayed up—and what they talked about (1:39). One of these disciples was Andrew. The name of the other is not given to us, but Bible scholars assume that it was John—the one who wrote this Gospel. They reason that humility kept him from mentioning his own name.

When a person finds Jesus, he usually wants his relatives to meet Him too (1:41). Salvation is too good to keep to oneself. So Andrew went quickly to his brother Simon with the thrilling news, "We have found the Messiah!" What an astounding announcement this was! For at least four thousand years, men had waited for the promised Christ, God's Anointed One. Now Simon hears from the lips of his own brother the startling news that the Messiah was nearby. Truly they were living where history was being made. How simple Andrew's message was. It was only five words—"We have found the Messiah"—yet God used it to win Simon. We do not have to be great preachers or clever speakers. We need only to tell men about the Lord Jesus in simple words, and God will take care of the rest.

Andrew brought his brother to the right place and to the right Person. What an important act that was! Because of Andrew's interest, Simon later became a great fisher of men, and one of the leading apostles of the Lord. Simon has received more publicity than his brother, but Andrew will doubtless share Peter's reward because it was Andrew who brought him to Jesus.

The Lord knew Simon's name without being told. He also knew that Simon had an unstable and timid character. And finally, He knew that Simon's character would be changed, so that he would be firm as a stone. How did Jesus know all this? Because He was and is God. Simon's name did change to Cephas (same as Peter), and he became a man of strong character, especially after the ascension of the Lord and the descent of the Holy Spirit.

## The Call of Philip and Nathanael (1:43-51)

This is now the fourth day we have read about in this chapter. The Lord walked northward into the region known as Galilee (1:43). There He found Philip and invited him to be a follower. "Follow me!" These are great words because of the One who spoke them and great because of the privilege they offered. The Savior is still issuing this simple, yet sublime invitation to all men everywhere.

Bethsaida was a city on the shores of the Sea of Galilee (1:44). Few cities in the world have ever been so honored. The Lord performed some of His mighty miracles there (Luke 10:13). It was the home of Philip, Andrew, and Peter. Yet it rejected the Savior, and as a result, it was destroyed so completely that we cannot tell now the exact spot where it was located.

Philip wanted to share his new-found joy with someone else, so he went and found Nathanael (1:45). His message was simple and to the point.

He told Nathanael that he had found the Messiah who had been foretold by Moses and the prophets—Jesus of Nazareth. Actually his message was not entirely accurate. He described Jesus as being the "son of Joseph." Jesus, of course, was born of the Virgin Mary but had no human father. Joseph adopted Jesus and thus became His legal father, though not His real father. J. S. Stewart says, "It never was Christ's way to demand a full-fledged faith for a beginning. It never was his way to hold men back from discipleship on the ground of an incomplete creed. And quite certainly that is not his way today. He puts himself alongside his brethren. He bids them attach themselves to him at any point they can. He takes them on with the faith that they can offer him. He is content with that as a beginning; and from that he leads his friends on, as he led the first group on, step by step, to the inmost secret of who he is and to the full glory of discipleship."

Nathanael had problems. Nazareth was a despised city of Galilee and it seemed impossible to him that the Messiah would live in such a poor neighborhood (1:46). And so he voiced the question that was in his mind. Philip did not argue. He felt that the best way to meet objections was to introduce men directly to the Lord Jesus—a valuable lesson for all who are seeking to win others to Christ. Don't argue. Don't engage in prolonged discussions. Just bid men to come and see.

Verse 47 shows that Jesus knew all things. Without any previous acquaintance with Nathanael, He declared him to be an Israelite in whom there was no trickery or deceit. Jacob had gained a reputation for methods that were not entirely honest. But Nathanael was an exception. He was an Israelite in whom there was no underhandedness. Nathanael was obviously surprised that a total Stranger should speak to him as if He had known him previously. Apparently he had been completely concealed when he was sitting under the fig tree. But Jesus saw him, even though he was so hidden. Perhaps it was the power of the Lord Jesus to see him when he was shut off from human view that convinced Nathanael. Or perhaps this knowledge was given to him in a supernatural way. In any event, he now knew that Jesus was the Son of God and the King of Israel.

The Lord had given Nathanael two proofs that He was the Messiah. He had described his character, and He had seen Nathanael when no other eyes could have seen him. These two proofs were sufficient for Nathanael, and he believed (1:50). But now the Lord Jesus promised that he would see greater proofs than these. He gave Nathanael a picture of the time in the future when He would come back to reign over all the earth. In that day, the heavens will be open. The favor of God will rest upon the King as He reigns, with Jerusalem as His capital. The angels of God will ascend and descend upon the Son of man. Angels are servants of God, traveling like flames of fire on His errands. When Jesus reigns as King, these angels will travel back and forth between heaven and earth, fulfilling His will. Jesus was saying to Nathanael that he had seen only very minor demonstrations of His Messiahship. In the future reign of Christ, he would see the Lord Jesus fully revealed as God's anointed Son. Then all mankind would know that Someone good did come out of Nazareth.

It is worth noting that when Jesus introduced a saying with the words "verily, verily," He notified us that what He was about to say was very important. The words mean "truly, truly," or "amen, amen."

## The First Sign: Water Changed to Wine (2:1-11)

The "third day" mentioned in this verse doubtless refers to the third day of the Lord Jesus' stay in Galilee. In verse 43 of chapter 1, you will remember, the Savior went into Galilee. We do not know exactly where Cana was situated, but we infer from verse 12 of this chapter that it was near Capernaum and on higher ground.

There was a marriage in Cana on this particular day, and the mother of Jesus was there. It is interesting to notice that Mary is spoken of as the mother of Jesus. The Savior was not famous because He was the son of the Virgin Mary, but she was well-known because she was the mother of our Lord. The Scriptures always give the preeminent place to Christ and not to Mary.

Jesus and His disciples were invited to the wedding (2:2). It was a wise decision on the part of those who arranged the marriage to invite Christ. So it is still a wise decision when people today invite the Lord to their marriage. In order to do this, of course, both bride and groom must be true believers in the Lord Jesus. Then, too, they must give their lives to the Savior and determine that their home will be a place where He loves to be.

The expression in verse 3 "they wanted wine" really means "they lacked wine"; the supply of wine had failed. When the mother of Jesus realized what had happened, she presented the problem to her Son. She knew that He could perform a miracle in order to provide wine, and doubtless she wanted her Son to reveal Himself to the assembled guests as the Son of

God. Wine in the Scriptures often speaks of joy. When Mary said, "They have no wine," she gave a very accurate description of men and women who have never been saved. There is no real, lasting joy for the unbeliever.

The reply of the Lord in verse 4, seems to us to be very cold and distant. But it is not as strong a rebuke as it would seem. The word "woman" used here is a title of respect, similar to our word "lady." When the Lord asked, "What have I to do with thee?" He indicated that in the performance of His divine mission, He was not subject to instructions from His mother, but acted entirely in obedience to the will of His Father in heaven.

The expression 'what have I to do with you,' (in the King James Version) occurs several times in the Bible. It means, 'What have we in common?' The answer implied is, 'Nothing.' David used it twice with respect to his cousins, the sons of Zeruiah, and Elisha used it in 2 Kings 3 to express how deep was the gulf between him and Jehoram the son of Ahab. Three times the demons, by using the same expression, reveal how Satan has nothing in common with Christ, or Christ with Satan. And the Lord used it to the Virgin Mary to show how impassable is the gulf between His sinless Deity and her sinful humanity, and that only One Voice had authority for His ear.

Mary had wanted to see Jesus glorified, but He must remind her that the time for this had not yet come. Before He would appear to the world as the all-conquering Christ, He must first ascend the altar of sacrifice, and this He did at the Cross of Calvary.

Mary understood the meaning of His words, and instructed the servants to do whatever He commanded them (2:5). She did not direct men to obey herself, or any other man. She pointed them to the Lord Jesus and told them that He was the One who should be obeyed. The teachings of the Lord Jesus are given to us in the pages of the New Testament. As we read this precious book, we should remember the last recorded words of Mary, "Do whatever he tells you."

In the place where the wedding was being held, there were six large stone vessels, containing between sixteen and twenty-seven gallons of water apiece (2:6). This water was used by the Jewish people for cleansing themselves from defilement. The Lord Jesus gave instructions that the waterpots should be filled with water. This the servants did immediately. The Lord Jesus used facilities that were available when He was about to perform a miracle. He allowed men to provide the waterpots, and to fill them with water, but then He did what no man could ever do—changed the water into wine! It was the servants and not the disciples who filled the vessels with water. Thus the Lord avoided the possibility of any charge of trickery. Also, the waterpots were filled to the brim, so that no one could say that wine had been added to the water.

The miracle having taken place, the Lord instructed the servants to draw out some of the contents of the vessels and to take these contents to the governor, or ruler, of the feast. From this, it is clear that the miracle had been instantaneous. The water did not become wine over a period of time, but in a second or so.

We read in verse 9 that the ruler of the feast was the one who had charge of arranging the tables and the food. When he had tasted the wine, he realized something unusual had happened! He did not know where it had come from, but he knew that the wine was of very high quality so he immediately began to inquire of the bridegroom.[2]

What should be the attitude of Christians toward wine today? Wine is sometimes prescribed for medicinal purposes, and this is entirely in accordance with the teaching of the New Testament (1 Timothy 5:23). However, because of the terrible abuses which have come in connection with the intemperate use of wine, most Christians will want to avoid it altogether. Anyone can become addicted to strong drink. The way to avert this danger is to leave liquor alone. Again, one must always consider the effect of his actions on others. Ordinarily, it would be a bad testimony for a Christian if an unsaved person should see him drinking wine, and for this reason he should abstain.

The ruler of the feast knew good wine when he tasted it. It is not possible that the beverage that was served to him was merely a form of grape juice (2:10). He would not have been impressed by that. On the contrary, he realized that this was no ordinary wine. His comments draw attention to the difference between the way the Lord Jesus acted and the way men commonly acted. The usual practice at a wedding was to serve the best wine at the first when men could best detect and enjoy the flavor of good wine. Later on they would not be as aware of the quality of their beverage. At this particular wedding, the best wine came last. There is a spiritual meaning in this for us. The world commonly offers men its best at the outset. It holds out its most attractive offers to young people. Then when they have wasted their lives in empty pleasure, the world has nothing but dregs for a person's old age. The Christian life is the very opposite. It gets better all the time. Christ keeps the best wine until the last.

This portion of Scripture has a very direct application to the Jewish nation. There was no true joy in Judaism any more. The people were going through a dreary round of rituals and ceremonies, but life for them was tasteless. They were strangers to divine joy. The Lord Jesus sought to teach them to put their faith in Him. He would turn their drab existence into fullness of joy. The water of Jewish ritual and ceremony could be turned into the wine of joyful reality in Christ.

The statement here in verse 11 that this was His beginning miracle rules out the silly miracles attributed to our Lord in His childhood found in such pseudo gospels as "The Gospel of Peter." They attribute to our Lord miracles performed when a child and are little short of blasphemous in character. Foreseeing this, the Holy Spirit safeguarded this period of our Lord's life and His character by this little additional note.

The changing of the water into wine was a sign, that is, a miracle with a significance. It was a super-human act with a spiritual meaning. The Lord's miracles also proved Jesus to be indeed the Christ of God.

By performing this sign, He manifested His glory. He revealed to men that He was indeed God, manifest in the flesh. His disciples believed on Him. Of course, in one sense they had believed on Him previously, but now their faith was strengthened, and they trusted Him more fully.

## At Jerusalem, Christ Cleanses the Temple (2:12-17)

The Savior now left Cana and went down to Capernaum with His mother, His brothers, and His disciples. They only stayed in Capernaum a few days. Soon after, the Lord went up to Jerusalem.

Beginning with verse 13 we have the Lord's first witness to the city of Jerusalem. It is worth noting that the Lord began and ended His public ministry by cleansing the temple at Passover time (compare Matthew 21:12, 13; Mark 11:15-18; Luke 19:45, 46). The Passover, of course, was an annual feast commemorating the time when the children of Israel were delivered from slavery in Egypt and were led through the Red Sea to the wilderness, and then to the promised land. The first celebration of the Passover is recorded in Exodus 12. Being a devout Jew, the Lord Jesus went up to Jerusalem for this important day in the calendar year.

Coming to the temple, He found it had become a market place (2:14). Oxen, sheep and doves were being sold there, and money changers were carrying on their business as well. The animals and birds were sold to the worshippers for use as sacrifices. The money changers took the money of those who came from foreign countries and changed it into the money of Jerusalem so that the pilgrims could pay the tax to the temple. It is likely that these money changers often took unfair advantage of those who traveled from great distances.

The scourge which the Lord made was probably a small lash made with strings. It is not recorded that He actually used it on anyone. Instead, it is probable that it was merely a symbol of authority which He held in His hand. Waving the scourge before Him, He cast the merchants out of the temple and upset the tables of the money changers. He commanded those who sold doves (the offering of the poor) to get out of the temple. It was not fitting that they should make a house of merchandise out of the house of God. In all ages, God has warned His people against using religious services as a means of getting rich. There was nothing cruel or unjust in any of these actions. Rather, they were simply an indication of His holiness and righteousness.

John records for us in verse 17 that when His disciples saw what was happening, they were reminded of Psalm 69:9 where it was predicted that when the Messiah came, He would he utterly consumed with a passion for the things of God. Now they saw Jesus manifesting an intense determination that the worship of God should be pure, and they realized that this was the One of whom the Psalmist had spoken.

We should remember that the Christian's body is the temple of the Holy Spirit. Just as the Lord Jesus was anxious that the temple in Jerusalem should be kept pure, so we should be careful that our bodies should be turned over to the Lord for continual cleansing.

## Jesus Foretells His Death and Resurrection (2:18-22)

The Jewish people always seemed to be seeking some sign or miracle from the Lord. However, the Lord Jesus performed one miracle after another, and yet their hearts were closed to Him. In verse 18 they questioned His right to cast the businessmen out of the temple. They demanded that He should perform some miracle to support His claim of being the Messiah. In answer, the Lord Jesus made an amazing statement concerning His death and resurrection. He told them they would destroy His sanctuary but in three days He would raise it up. The deity of the Lord Jesus is again seen in this verse. Only God could say, "In three days I will raise it up." The Jews did not understand Him. They were more interested in material things than in spiritual truth. The only temple they could think about was the temple of Herod which was then standing in Jerusalem. It had taken forty-six years to build this temple, and they could not see how any man could possibly rebuild it in three days. The Lord Jesus, however, was speaking about His own body, which was the sanctuary in which all the fullness of the Godhead dwelt. Just as these Jews had defiled the temple in Jerusalem, so they would put Him to death in a few short years. Later on, after the Lord Jesus had been crucified and was raised from the dead, His disciples remembered He had promised to rise again in three days. With such a marvelous fulfillment of prophecy before their eyes, they believed the Scripture, and the word which Jesus had spoken.

We often come across truths in the Bible which are difficult to understand. But we learn here that we should treasure the Word of God in our hearts. Some day later the Lord will make it plain to us, even though we do not understand it now. When it says in this verse that they believed the Scripture, it means that they believed the Old Testament predictions concerning the resurrection of the Lord Jesus.

## Many Profess to Believe on Christ (2:23-25)

As the result of the miracles which Jesus performed in Jerusalem at the time of the Passover, many believed on Him—that is they professed to accept Him. There was no reality to their action; it was merely an outward display of following Jesus. It was similar to what we have in the world today where many claim to be Christians who have never truly been born again through faith in the Lord Jesus Christ.

Although many believed in Him (2:23), yet Jesus did not believe in them. He did not trust Himself to them. He realized that they were coming to Him out of curiosity. They were looking for something sensational and spectacular. "He knew all men." He knew their thoughts and their motives. He knew why they acted the way they did. He knew whether their faith was real or only an imitation. No one knew the heart of man better than the Lord Himself.

He did not need anyone to teach Him or enlighten Him on this subject. He had full knowledge of what was in man and why man behaved as he did.

## Jesus Teaches Nicodemus about the New Birth (3:1-21)

The story of Nicodemus is in contrast with what has just gone before. Many of the Jews professed to believe on the Lord, but He knew their faith was not genuine. Nicodemus was an exception. The Lord recognized in him an earnest desire to know the truth. Verse 1 should begin with the word "but." "But there was a man of the Pharisees named Nicodemus, a ruler of the Jews." He was recognized as a teacher among his people. Perhaps he came to the Lord for instruction, so that he might return to the Jews with this additional learning.

The Bible does not say why Nicodemus came to Jesus by night. The most obvious explanation is that he would have been embarrassed to be seen going to Jesus, since the Lord had by no means been accepted by the majority of the Jewish people. However, he did come to Jesus. Nicodemus acknowledged the Lord to be a teacher sent by God, since no one could perform such miracles without the direct help of God. But, learned though he was, Nicodemus did not recognize Jesus as God manifest in flesh. He was like so many today who say Jesus was a great man, a wonderful teacher, an outstanding example. All of these statements fall very far short of the full truth. Jesus was and is God.

At first sight, the response of the Lord in verse 3 does not seem to be connected with what Nicodemus had said. But it seems the Lord Jesus was saying, "Nicodemus, you have come to Me for teaching, but what you really need is to be born again. That is where you must begin. You must be born from above. Otherwise, you can never see the kingdom of God."

As a Jew, Nicodemus had been looking for the Messiah to come and free the nation of Israel from the bondage of Rome. Nicodemus longed for the time when the Messiah would set up His kingdom on the earth, when the Jewish people would be chief among the nations, and when all their enemies would be destroyed. Now the Lord informed Nicodemus that in order to enter this kingdom, a man must be born again. Just as the first birth is necessary for physical life, so a second birth is necessary for divine life. (The expression "born again" may also mean "born from above.") In other words, Christ's kingdom can only be entered by those whose lives have been changed. Since His reign will be a righteous one, His subjects must be righteous also. He could not reign over people who were going on in their sins.

Here again we see how difficult it was for men to understand the words of the Lord Jesus. Nicodemus insisted on taking everything in a literal sense (3:4). He could not understand how a grown-up man could be born again. He pondered the physical impossibility of a man entering into his mother's womb again in order to be born (1 Corinthians 2:14). In further explanation, the Lord Jesus told Nicodemus that he must be born of water and of the Spirit. Otherwise, he could never enter into the kingdom of God.

What did the Lord Jesus mean? Many insist that the Lord Jesus spoke of the necessity of baptism for salvation. However, such a teaching is contrary to the rest of the Bible. Throughout the Word of God we read that salvation is by faith in the Lord Jesus Christ alone. Baptism is intended for those who have already been saved, but not as a means of salvation.

Some suggest that the water in verse 5 refers to the Word of God. In Ephesians 5:25-26, water is closely associated with the Word of God. Also, in 1 Peter 1:23, the new birth is said to take place through the Word of God. It is quite possible, therefore, that water in this verse does refer to the Bible. There can be no salvation apart from the Scriptures. The message contained in the Word of God must be appropriated by the sinner before there can be the new birth.

But water may also refer to the Holy Spirit. In John 7:38-39, the Lord Jesus spoke of rivers of living water, and we are distinctly told that when He used the word *water* He was speaking of the Holy Spirit. If water means the Spirit in chapter 7, why can it not have the same meaning here in chapter 3? If water is taken to mean the Spirit, then it would appear on the surface that the Spirit is mentioned twice in this verse. But the word translated "and" could just as correctly have been translated "even." Thus, the verse might read, "Except a man be born of water, even the Spirit, he cannot enter into the kingdom of God." We believe that this is the correct meaning of the verse. Physical birth is not enough. There must also be spiritual birth if a man is to enter the kingdom of God. This spiritual birth is produced by the Holy Spirit of God when a person believes on the Lord Jesus Christ. This interpretation is supported by the expression "born of the Spirit" found twice in the verses 6 and 8.

Even if Nicodemus could in some way have entered into his mother's womb a second time and been born a second time, that would not have corrected the evil nature in him. The expression "that which is born of the flesh is flesh" means that children born of human parents are born in sin and are hopeless and helpless as far as saving themselves is concerned. On the other hand, "that which is born of the Spirit is spirit." A spiritual birth takes place when a person trusts in the Lord Jesus. When a man is born again through the Spirit, he receives a new nature, and is made fit for the kingdom of God.

Nicodemus was not to be amazed by the teachings of the Lord Jesus. He must realize that a man must be born again. He must understand the inability of human nature to remedy its fallen condition. He must realize that in order to be a subject of God's kingdom, a man must be holy, pure, and spiritual.

As He so often did, the Lord Jesus used nature to illustrate spiritual truth. He reminded Nicodemus, in verse 8, that the wind blows wherever it wishes, and a man can hear its sound, but he cannot tell where it comes from or where it is going. The new birth is very much like the wind. First of all, it takes place according to the will of God. It is not a power which man holds in his own control. Secondly, the new birth is invisible. You cannot see it taking place, but you can see the results of it in a man's life. When a man has been saved, a change comes over him. The evil things which he formerly loved, he now hates. The things of God which he formerly despised, these things are now the very things which he loves. Just as no one can fully understand the wind, so the new birth is a miraculous work of the Spirit of God which man is not able to comprehend fully. Moreover the new birth, like the wind, is unpredictable. It is not possible to state just when and where it will take place.

Again, in verse 9, Nicodemus illustrated the inability of the natural mind to enter into divine things. Doubtless he was still trying to think of the new birth as a natural or physical event, rather than as a spiritual one. And so he asked the Lord Jesus, "How can these things be?" The Lord Jesus stated in verse 10 that as the teacher of Israel, Nicodemus should have understood these things. The Old Testament Scriptures clearly taught that when the Lord Jesus came back to the earth to set up His kingdom, He would first judge His enemies and destroy all things that offend. Only those who had confessed and forsaken their sins would enter into the kingdom. The Lord Jesus then underlined the infallibility of His teaching, and man's unbelief concerning it. From all eternity, He had known the truthfulness of this and had only taught what He knew and had seen. But Nicodemus and most of the Jews of his day refused to believe His testimony.

What were the earthly things to which the Lord referred in verse 12? It was His earthly kingdom. As a student of the Old Testament Scriptures, Nicodemus knew that one day the Messiah would come and set up a literal kingdom upon the earth with Jerusalem as His capital. What Nicodemus failed to understand was that in order to enter this kingdom, there must be a new birth. What then were the heavenly things to which the Lord referred? They are the truths which are explained in the following verses—the wonderful way by which a person receives this new birth.

Only one person was qualified to speak about heavenly things, since He was the only One who was in heaven (3:13). The Lord Jesus was not merely a human teacher sent from God, but He was One who lived with God the Father from all eternity, and came down into the world. When He said that "no man has ascended up to heaven," He did not mean that Old Testament saints such as Enoch and Elijah had not gone to heaven, but that no human being had access to the presence of God continually in the way in which He had it. He could ascend to God's dwelling place in a unique way because He had descended out of heaven to this earth. Even as the Lord Jesus stood on earth, speaking with Nicodemus, He said that He was in heaven. How could this be? As God, the Lord was in all places at one and the same time. This is what we mean when we say that He is omnipresent.

The Lord Jesus had already told Nicodemus in verse 14 that the new birth was necessary. But how can the new birth take place? The penalty of man's sins must be met. Man cannot go to heaven in his sins. Just as Moses had lifted up a serpent of brass on a pole in the wilderness when all the children of Israel had been bitten by serpents, so must the Son of Man be lifted up. (Read Numbers 21:4-9.) In Moses' day many of the sinning Israelites had died when bitten by the serpents. When the survivors cried to the Lord in repentance, the Lord told Moses to make a serpent of brass and put it on a pole. The bitten Israelite who looked to the serpent was miraculously healed. The Lord Jesus quoted this incident to illustrate how the new birth takes place. Men and women have been bitten by the viper of sin and are condemned to eternal death. The serpent of brass was a picture of the Lord Jesus. Brass, in the Bible, speaks of judgment. The Lord Jesus was sinless and should never have been punished, but He took our place and bore the judgment which we deserved. The pole speaks of the Cross of

Calvary upon which the Lord Jesus was lifted up. We are saved by looking to Him in faith. The Lord Jesus was made sin for us, He who knew no sin, that we might be made the righteousness of God in Him. Whoever believes on the Lord Jesus Christ receives eternal life as a free gift.

John chapter 3, verse 16 is one of the best known verses in the entire Bible, doubtless because it states the gospel so clearly and simply. It summarizes what the Lord Jesus had been teaching Nicodemus concerning the manner by which the new birth was received. "God," we read, "so loved the world." The world here includes all mankind. God does not love men's sins or the wicked world system, but He loves people and is not willing that any should perish. The extent of His love is shown by the fact that He gave His only begotten (unique) Son. God has no other Son like the Lord Jesus. It was an expression of His infinite love that He would be willing to give the only Son He had for a race of rebel sinners. This does not mean that everyone is saved. A person must receive what Christ has done for him before God will give him eternal life. Therefore, the words are added, "that whosoever believeth in him should not perish." There is no need for anyone to perish. A way has been provided whereby all might be saved, but a person must acknowledge Jesus Christ to be his Lord and Savior. When he does this, he has eternal life as a present possession.

God is not a harsh, cruel ruler, anxious to pour out His anger on mankind (3:17). God's heart is filled with tenderness toward man and He has gone to the utmost cost in order to save men. He could have sent His Son into the world to condemn the world, but instead He sent Him to suffer, bleed, and die that the world might be saved through Him. The work of the Lord Jesus Christ on the Cross of Calvary was of such tremendous value that all sinners everywhere could be saved if they would receive Him.

Men are either believers or unbelievers. Verse 18 tells us that our eternal destiny is determined by the attitude we take toward the Son of God. The one who trusts the Savior is not condemned, but the one who does not trust Him is condemned already. The Lord Jesus has finished the work of salvation, and now it is up to each individual to decide whether he will accept Him or reject Him. It is a terrible thing to reject such a gift of love. If a man will not believe on the Lord Jesus, God can do nothing else but condemn him. "Believing in His name" is the same as believing in Him. In the Bible, the name stands for the person. If you trust His name, you trust Himself.

Jesus was the Light who came into the world (3:19). He was the sinless, spotless Lamb of God. He died for the sins of the entire world. But do men love Him for this? No—they resent Him. They prefer their sins to having Jesus as Savior, and so they reject Him. Just as some creeping things scurry away from the light, so wicked men flee from the presence of Christ. Those who love sin hate the light, because the light exposes their sinfulness. When the Lord Jesus was here in the world, sinful men were made uncomfortable by His presence because He revealed their awful condition by His own holiness. The best way to reveal the crookedness of one stick is to place a straight stick beside it. Coming into the world as a perfect Man, the Lord Jesus revealed the crookedness of all other men, by comparison. If a man is truly honest before God, he will come to the Light, that is, to the Lord Jesus, realize his own utter worthlessness and sinfulness and trust the Savior for himself and thus be born again through faith in Christ.

## The Ministry of John the Baptist in Judea (3:22-36)

The Lord's witness in the city of Jerusalem has been described. From verse 22 to the end of the chapter, we have Christ testifying in Judea where doubtless He continued to proclaim the good news of salvation. As men came to the light, they were baptized. It would appear from this verse that Jesus Himself did the baptizing, but we learn in John 4:2 that it was done by His disciples.

The John referred to in verse 23 is John the Baptist. He was still preaching his message of repentance in the region of Judea and baptizing those Jews who were willing to repent in preparation for the coming of the Messiah. John was baptizing in Aenon because there was much water there. This does not prove conclusively that he baptized by immersion, but it certainly strongly implies as much. If he baptized by sprinkling or pouring, there would have been no necessity of having much water.

Verse 24 is given in explanation of John's continued ministry and of the continued response of devout Jews to it. In the near future, John would be cast into prison and beheaded for his faithful testimony. But in the meantime, he was still diligently carrying out his commission.

From verse 25 it is clear that John's disciples became engaged in a dispute with a certain Jew about "purifying." The word "purifying" here refers to baptism. The argument was whether the baptism of John was better than that of Jesus. Which baptism had the greater power? Which was of the greater value? Perhaps some of John's disciples unwisely contended that no baptism could be better than that of their master. Perhaps one of the Pharisees tried to make John's disciples jealous of Jesus and His current popularity. They came to John for a decision. They seemed to be saying to him, "If your baptism is the better, why is it that so many men are leaving you and going to Christ?" (The expression "he that was with thee beyond Jordan" refers to Jesus.) John bore witness to the Lord Jesus, and as a result of this witness, many of John's own disciples left him and began to follow Jesus.

There are two explanations of John's reply. If he was referring to the Lord Jesus, it means that any success the Savior received was an indication of God's approval on Him. If John was referring to himself, he was saying that he had never pretended to be any one great or important. He had never claimed that his baptism was superior to that of Jesus. He simply said here that he did not have anything but what he had received from heaven. That is true of all of us and there is no reason in the world why we should be proud or seek to build up ourselves in men's esteem.

John reminded his disciples, in verse 28, that he had pointed out time and again that he was not the Christ, but was simply sent to prepare the way for the Messiah. Why should they argue over him? Why should they seek to form a party around him? He was not the important one, but was simply trying to point men to the Lord Jesus.

The Lord Jesus Christ was the bridegroom. John the Baptist was merely the friend of the Bridegroom. Perhaps we would say today that he was the "best man." The bride does not belong to the friend of the bridegroom, but rather to the bridegroom himself. Therefore, it was fitting that the people should follow Jesus rather than John. The bride here refers in a general way to all who would become disciples of the Lord Jesus. In the Old Testament, Israel was spoken of as the wife of Jehovah. Later on in the New Testament, those who are members of Christ's Church are described under the figure of a bride. But here in John's Gospel, the word was used in a general sense to include those who left John the Baptist when the Messiah appeared. It did not mean either Israel or the Church. John was not unhappy to lose followers. It was his great joy to listen to the voice of the Bridegroom. He was satisfied that Jesus be given all the attention. His joy was fulfilled when Christ was praised and honored by men.

The entire object of John's ministry is summarized in verse 30. He labored ceaselessly to point men and women to the Lord, and to make them realize His true worth. To do this he must keep himself in the background.

For a servant of Christ to seek to attract attention to himself is really a form of disloyalty. Note the three "musts" in this chapter—for the Sinner (3:7); for the Savior (3:14); and for the Saint (3:30).

Jesus is the One who came from above and is above all. This statement in verse 31 shows His heavenly origin and supreme position. To prove his own inferiority, John the Baptist said that he himself was of the earth and was earthly and spoke of the earth. This simply meant that, as to his birth, he was born a man of human parents. He had no heavenly rank and could not speak with the same authority as the Son of God. He was inferior to the Lord Jesus because "he that cometh from above is above all." Christ is the supreme Sovereign of the universe. It is only proper, therefore, that men should follow Him rather than His messenger. But when the Lord Jesus spoke in verse 32, He spoke with authority. He told men of what He had seen and heard. There was no possibility of error or deceit. Yet strange to say no man received His testimony. The expression "no man" is not to be taken in an absolute sense. There were individual men here and there who did accept the words of the Lord Jesus. However, John was looking at mankind in general and simply stating that the Savior's teachings were rejected by most. Jesus was the One who came down from heaven, but comparatively few were willing to listen to Him.

Verse 33 describes the few who did accept the words of the Lord as being the very words of God. By their acceptance, they were setting their seal to this, that God is true. So it is today. When men accept the message of the gospel, they take sides with God against themselves and against the rest of mankind. They realize that if God has said something, it must be true. Notice how clearly this verse teaches the deity of Christ. It says that whoever believes the testimony of Christ acknowledges that God is true. This is just another way of saying that the testimony of Christ is the testimony of God, and to receive the one is to receive the other also.

Jesus was the One whom God sent. He spoke the words of God. To support this statement, John stated that God did not give the Spirit by measure to Him. The Lord Jesus Christ was anointed by the Holy Spirit of God in a way that was not true of any other person. Others have been conscious of the help of the Holy Spirit in their ministry, but no one else ever had such a Spirit-filled ministry as the Son of God.

Verse 35 records one of the seven times in John's Gospel where we are told that the Father loves the Son. Here that love is manifested in giving Him control over all things. Among these things over which the Lord Jesus has complete charge are the destinies of men, as explained in the following verse. God has given Christ the power to grant everlasting life to all who believe on Him. This is one of the clearest verses in all the Bible on how a person can be saved. Salvation is not by keeping the law, obeying the Golden Rule, doing the best we can, or working our way to heaven. It is simply by believing on the Son. Remember God is speaking. He is making a promise that can never be broken. He says, clearly and distinctly, that anyone who believes on His Son has everlasting life. To accept this promise is not a leap in the dark. It is simply believing what could not possibly be false. Those who do not obey the Son of God will not see life, but the wrath of God abides on them already. From this verse we learn that our eternal destiny depends upon what we do with the Son of God. If we receive Him, God gives us eternal life as a free gift. If we reject Him, we will never enjoy everlasting life, and not only so, but God's wrath already hangs over us, ready to fall at any moment.

CHAPTER

# 3

# A Bad Woman and a Good Man (John 4)

In chapters 3 and 4 we have our Lord's conversations with two different individuals, Nicodemus and the woman of Samaria. The following are some of the striking contrasts to be seen between these two:

| **Nicodemus** | **The Woman of Samaria** |
| --- | --- |
| A good man | An evil woman |
| A leader of the Jews | An outcast of the Samaritans |
| Came by night | Was found at mid-day |
| Seeking the Savior | Sought by the Savior |
| Had a knowledge of God—"We know . . ." | Was ignorant of the truth—" . . . you know not . . ." |
| The New Birth | Worship |
| No apparent result | An immediate result |

## The Conversion of a Woman of Samaria (4:1-30)

In verses 1 to 3 we read that the Pharisees had heard that Jesus was baptizing more disciples than John and that John's popularity was evidently declining. Perhaps they had attempted to use this fact to stir up jealousy and contention between the disciples of John and those of the Lord Jesus. Actually, the Lord Jesus Himself did not perform the act of baptism. This was done by His disciples. However, the people were baptized as followers or disciples of the Lord. By leaving Judea and journeying into Galilee, Jesus would prevent the Pharisees from being successful in their efforts to cause divisions. But there is something else of significance in this verse. Judea was the headquarters of the Jewish people, whereas Galilee was known as a Gentile region. The Lord Jesus realized that the Jewish people were already rejecting Him and His testimony, and so here He turns to the Gentile people with the message of salvation.

Samaria was on the direct route from Judea to Galilee (4:4). But few Jews ever took this direct route. The region of Samaria was so despised by the Jewish people that they often took a very roundabout route through Perea in order to get north into Galilee. Thus, when it says that the Lord Jesus must needs go through Samaria, the thought is not so much that He was compelled to do so by geographical considerations, but rather by the fact that there was a needy soul in Samaria to whom He could be of help. Traveling into Samaria, the Lord Jesus came to a little village named Sychar (4:5). Not far from that village was a piece of ground which Jacob had given to his son Joseph, as recorded in Genesis 48:22. As the Lord Jesus journeyed over this territory, all the scenes of its past history were constantly before His mind. A spring known as Jacob's well was in this area. It is one of the few Biblical sites which can be identified quite positively today.

It was about noontime (the sixth hour) when the Lord Jesus reached the well. He was weary as a result of His long walk so He sat down on the well. Although Jesus is God, the Son, He is also a Man. As God, He could never become weary, but as Man, He did. We find difficulty in understanding these things. But the Person of the Lord Jesus Christ can never be fully understood by any mortal mind. The truth that God could come down into the world and live as a Man among men is a mystery which passes our understanding.

As the Lord Jesus was sitting by the well, a woman came out from the village to draw water (4:7). Noon was a very unusual time for women to go to the well for water; it was the hottest part of the day. But this woman was a very wicked sinner, and she may have chosen this time because she knew that there would be no other women there to see her. Of course, the Lord Jesus knew all along that she would be at the well at this time. He knew that she was a soul in need, and so He determined to meet her and to rescue her from her sinful life.

In verse 7 and the verses to follow, we find the master Soul Winner at work, and we will do well to study the methods He used to bring this woman to a sense of her need and to offer her the solution to her problem. Our Lord spoke to the woman just seven times. The woman spoke seven times also—

six times to the Lord and once to the men of the city. Perhaps if we spoke to the Lord as much as she did, we might have the success in testimony that she had when she spoke to the men of the city. The Lord opened the conversation by asking a favor. Wearied with His journey, He desired a drink. His disciples had gone to Sychar to purchase some food and to all outward appearance, the Lord had no means for getting water from the well (4:8).

The woman recognized Jesus as a Jew and was amazed that He would speak to her, a Samaritan (4:9). The Samaritans claimed descent from Jacob, and looked upon themselves as true Israelites. Actually they were of mixed Jewish and heathen descent. Mount Gerizim had been adopted by them as their official place of worship. This was a mountain in Samaria, clearly visible to the Lord and to this woman as they talked together. The Jewish people had a deep dislike for the Samaritans. They considered them half-breeds. That is why this woman said, "How is it that you, being a Jew, ask a drink of me, which am a woman of Samaria?" Little did she realize that she was speaking to her Creator, and that His love rose above all the petty distinctions of men.

We see in verse 10 that by asking a favor, the Lord had aroused her interest and curiosity. He aroused them still further by speaking of Himself as both God and Man. He was first of all the gift of God—the One God gave to be the Savior of the world, His only begotten Son. But He was also a Man— the One who, wearied with His journey, asked her for a drink. In other words, if she had realized that the One to whom she was talking was God manifest in the flesh, she would have asked Him for a blessing, and He would have given her living water. From verse 11 we see the woman could only think of literal water and of the impossibility of His getting it without the necessary equipment. She completely failed to recognize the Lord, or to understand His words.

Her confusion deepened when she thought of the patriarch Jacob, who had given this well (4:12). He, himself, had used it, as well as his children and his cattle. Now here was a weary traveler, centuries later, who asked for a drink from Jacob's well and yet who claimed to be able to give something better than the water which Jacob had given. If He had something better, why should He ask for water from Jacob's well? So the Lord began to explain the difference between the literal water of Jacob's well and the water which He would give. Whoever drank of this water would thirst again. Surely the Samaritan woman could understand this. She had been coming out day after day to draw from the well; yet the need was never completely met. And so it is with all the wells of this world. Men seek their pleasure and satisfaction in earthly things, but these things are not able to quench the thirst of the heart of man.

The water which Jesus gives truly satisfies (4:14). Those who drink of Christ's blessings and mercies shall never thirst again. Not only do His benefits fill the heart, but they overflow it as well. They are a bubbling fountain, constantly overflowing, not only in this life but in eternity as well. The contrast is very vivid. All that earth can provide is not sufficient to fill the human heart. But the blessings which Christ provides not only fill the heart, but they are too great for any heart to contain. The pleasures of this world are for a few short years, but the pleasures which Christ provides go on into everlasting life.

When the woman heard of this marvelous water, she immediately wanted it. But she was still thinking of literal water. She did not want to have to come out to the well every day to draw the water and to carry it home on her head in a heavy pot. She did not realize that the water of which the Lord Jesus had been speaking was spiritual, that He was referring to all the blessings which come to a human soul through faith in Him.

But in verse 16 there is an abrupt change in the conversation here. She had just asked for the water, and the Lord Jesus told her to go and call her husband. Why? Because before this woman could be saved, she must acknowledge herself a sinner. She must come to Christ in true repentance, confessing her guilt and shame. The Lord Jesus knew all about the sinful life she had lived, and He was going to lead her, step by step, to see it for herself.

Only those who know themselves to be lost can be saved. All men are lost, but not all are willing to admit it. In seeking to win men for Christ, we must never avoid the sin question. Men must face the fact that they are dead in trespasses and in sins, need a Savior, and cannot save themselves and that Jesus is the Savior they need, and will save them if they confess their sin and trust in Him.

We see in verse 17 that at first the woman tried to withhold the truth without telling a lie. She said, "I have no husband." Perhaps in a strictly legal sense, her statement was true but she was trying to hide the fact that she was living in sin with a man who was not her husband. The Lord Jesus, as God, knew all this. This is why He says in verse 18, "You are right in saying, 'I have no husband.'" He knew all about her. The Lord never used His knowledge to needlessly expose or shame a person. But He did use it, as here, in order to deliver a person from the bondage of sin. How startled she must have been when He recited her past history! She had had five husbands, and the man with whom she was now living was not her husband.

There is some difference of opinion among Bible students about this verse. Some teach that the woman's five previous husbands had either died or had deserted her, and that there was nothing sinful in her relationships with them. Whether or not this is so, it is clear from the latter part of the verse that this woman was an adulteress. "He whom thou now hast is not thy husband." This is the important point. The woman was a sinner, and until she was willing to acknowledge this, the Lord could not bless her with the living water.

With her life laid open before her, the woman realized the One speaking to her was no ordinary person. However, she did not realize yet that He was God. She thought He was a prophet, that is, a spokesman for God (4:19).

It seems now that the woman had become convicted of her sins, and so she tried to change the subject by introducing a question concerning the proper place for worship. "Our fathers worshiped on this mountain," she said, pointing to Mount Gerizim. Then she reminded the Lord (unnecessarily) that the Jewish people claimed Jerusalem as the proper place of worship. The Lord Jesus did not avoid her comment, but used it to impart further spiritual truth. He told her that the time was coming when neither Jerusalem nor Gerizim would be the place of worship. In the Old Testament, Jerusalem was appointed by God as *the* city where worship should be offered to Him. The temple in Jerusalem was the dwelling place of God, and devout Jews came to Jerusalem with their sacrifices and offerings. Of course, in the gospel age, this is no longer so. God does not have any certain place on earth where men must go to worship. The Lord explained this more fully in the verses to follow.

When the Lord said in verse 22, "You worship what you do not know," He condemned the Samaritan mode of worship. This is in marked contrast with religious teachers who say all religions are good and all lead to heaven at last. The Lord Jesus informed this woman that the worship of the Samaritans was not authorized by God, neither was it approved by Him. It had been invented by man and carried on without the sanction of the Word of God. This was not so with the worship of the Jews. The Jewish people were His chosen earthly people. He had given them instructions on the way to worship Him. "Salvation is from the Jews," said the Lord. The Jewish people were appointed by God to be His messengers, and it was to them the Scriptures had been given. Also, it was through the Jewish nation the Messiah was given. He was born of a Jewish mother.

Next the Lord informed the woman that, with His coming, God no longer had a certain place on earth for worship (4:23). Those who believe on the Lord Jesus can worship God at any time and in any place. True worship means that no matter where he is, a believer can enter the presence of God by faith and praise and worship Him. Jesus told this woman that time on worship of the Father would be in spirit and in truth. The Jews had reduced worship to outward forms and ceremonies. But theirs was not a worship of the spirit. It was outward, not inward. Their bodies might be bowed down on the ground but their hearts were not right before God. They were worshipping as far as outward appearance was concerned, but it was not spiritual worship.

The Samaritans, on the other hand, had a form of worship which was even more false. It had no Scriptural authority at all. They had started their own religion and were carrying out ordinances of their own invention. Thus, when the Lord Jesus said that worship must be in spirit and in truth, He was rebuking both Jews and Samaritans. But He was also informing them that, now that He had come, it was possible for men to draw near to God through Him in true and sincere worship. The Father "seeks such to worship him." Ponder this! The Father seeks worshippers. God is interested in the adoration of His people. Does He receive this from me?

The first part of verse 24 might also be translated "God is Spirit." This is a definition of God's being. He is not a mere man, subject to all the errors and limitations of humanity. Neither is He confined to any one place at any time. He is an invisible Person who is present in all places at one and the same time, who is all-knowing, and who is all-powerful. He is perfect in all His ways. Therefore, those who worship Him must worship Him in spirit and in truth. There must be no sham or hypocrisy. There must be no pretense of being religious, when inwardly one's life is corrupt. There must be no idea that in going through a series of rituals, God is thereby pleased. Even if God instituted those rituals Himself, He still insists that man approach Him with a broken and a contrite heart. Two more "musts" are found in this chapter—a "must" for the Winner of souls (4:4) and a "must" for the Worshipper (4:24).

As the woman of Samaria had listened to the Lord, she had been made to think of the coming Messiah (4:25). The Spirit of God had stirred up within her a desire that the Messiah should come. She expressed confidence that when He did come, He would teach all things. In this statement, she showed a very clear understanding of one of the great purposes of Christ's coming.

What the Lord Jesus really said to her in reply was, "I who speak to you am he." The word "he" is not a part of the original text. The sentence might perhaps be clearer with the word *he* included, yet there is a deep significance to the actual words of the Lord. He used one of the names which God applied to Himself in the Old Testament. He said, "I AM is speaking unto you," or, in other words, "Jehovah is the one who is speaking unto you." He was announcing to her the startling truth that the One who was speaking to her was the Messiah for whom she had been looking and that He was also God Himself. The Jehovah of the Old Testament is the Jesus of the New Testament.

When the disciples returned from Sychar they found Jesus talking with this woman (4:27). They were surprised He would speak with her, for she was a Samaritan. Also, they could possibly discern she was a sinful woman. Yet no one asked the Lord what He was seeking from the woman or why He was speaking with her. It has been well said, "The disciples marvel that He talks with the woman; they would have been better employed wondering that He talked with them!"

The woman left her waterpot! It symbolized the things she had used to satisfy her deepest longings. They all had failed. Now that she had found the Lord Jesus, she had no more need for the things which had formerly been so prominent in her life.

> "I tried the broken cisterns, Lord,
> But ah! the waters failed!
> E'en as I stooped to drink, they fled,
> And mocked me as I wailed."
>
> "Now none but Christ can satisfy,
> None other name for me;
> There's love, and life, and lasting joy,
> Lord Jesus, found in Thee."

She not only left her waterpot but she went into the city. Whenever a person is saved, he immediately begins to think of others who are in need of the water of life. J. Hudson Taylor said, "Some are jealous to be successors of the Apostles; I would rather be a successor of the Samaritan woman, who, while they went for food, forgot her waterpot in her zeal for souls."

We see from verse 29 that her witness was simple but effective. She invited the townspeople to come and see the Man who told her all that she ever did. Also, she aroused within their hearts the possibility that this Man might indeed be the Messiah. In the Revised Version, the latter part of this verse reads, "Can this be the Christ?" In her own mind, there could be little doubt because He had already announced Himself to her as the Christ. But she raised the question in their minds so that they might go to Jesus and find out for themselves. Doubtless this woman was well known in the village for her sin and shame. How startling it must have been for the people to see her standing in the public places now, bearing public witness to the Lord Jesus Christ! The testimony of the woman was effective. The people left their homes and their work and began to go out to find Jesus.

## Christ's Great Delight in Doing God's Will (4:31-38)

Now that the disciples were back, they encouraged the Lord to eat. Apparently they were not aware of the momentous events that were taking place. At this historic moment when a Samaritan city was being introduced to the Lord of Glory, their thoughts could rise no higher than food for their bodies (4:32). The Lord Jesus had found His nourishment and support in winning worshippers to His Father. Compared to this joy, physical food was of little importance to Him. We get what we go after in life. The disciples were interested in food. They went into the village to get food. They came back with it. The Lord was interested in souls. He was interested in saving men and women from sin, and giving them the water of everlasting life. He, too, found what He went after. What are we interested in?

Because of their earthly outlook, the disciples failed to understand the meaning of the Lord's words. They did not appreciate the fact that the joy and happiness of spiritual success can for the time lift men above all bodily wants, and supply the place of material meat and drink. And so they concluded that someone must have come along and given food to the Lord Jesus (4:34). A gain the Lord Jesus tried to turn their attention from the material to the spiritual. His food was to do the will of God, and to finish the work which God had given Him to do. Not that the Lord Jesus refrained from eating food, but rather the great aim and object of His life was to do the will of God.

Perhaps the disciples had been talking together about the coming harvest (4:35). Or perhaps it was a common saying among the Jews, "Four months between seed time and harvest." At any rate, the Lord Jesus used the physical fact of harvest to teach a spiritual lesson. The disciples should not think that harvest time was still in the distance. They could not afford to spend their lives in quest of food and clothing, with the thought that God's work could be done later on. They must realize that the fields were already white unto harvest. The fields here, of course, refer to the world. At the very moment when the Lord spoke these words, He was in the midst of a harvest field containing the souls of Samaritan men and women. He was telling the disciples that a great work of in-gathering lay before them, and that they should give themselves to it immediately and diligently. So today, the Lord would say to believers, "Lift up your eyes, and look on the fields." As we spend time contemplating the great need of the world, the Lord will lay upon our hearts a burden for the lose souls about us. Then it will be up to us to go forth for Him, seeking to bring in the sheaves of ripened grain.

In verse 36 we find the Lord Jesus now instructing the disciples concerning the work to which they were called. He had chosen them to be reapers. They would not only earn wages in this life, but they would gather fruit for eternity as well. Service for Christ has many rewards at the present time. But in a coming day, reapers will have the additional joy of seeing souls in heaven because of their faithfulness in proclaiming the gospel message. In heaven, both the sower and the reaper will rejoice together. In natural life, the field must first be prepared for the seed, and then the seed must be sown in it. Later on, the grain is harvested. Thus it is in the spiritual life also. First of all, the message must be preached, then it must be watered with prayer. But when the harvest season comes, all who have had a part in the work rejoice together.

In this, the Lord saw a fulfillment of the proverb that was common in that day, "One sows and another reaps." Some Christians are called upon to preach the gospel for many years without seeing very much fruit for their labor. Others step in at the end of those years, and many souls turn to the Lord. The Lord Jesus was sending His disciples into areas that had areas that had already been prepared by others. Throughout the Old Testament period, the prophets had foretold the coming of the gospel era and of the Messiah. Then, too, John the Baptist came as a forerunner of the Lord, seeking to prepare the hearts of the people to receive Him. The Lord Himself had sown the seed in Samaria, and prepared a harvest for the reapers. Now the disciples were about to step into the harvest field, and the Lord wanted them to know that, while they would have the joy of seeing many turning to Christ, they should understand they were entering into the labors of other men. Very few souls are ever saved through the ministry of a single person. Most people hear the gospel many times before they accept the Savior. Therefore, the one who finally leads a person to Christ should not exalt himself as if he were the only instrument God used in this marvelous work.

## Many Samaritans Believe on Jesus (4:39-42)

As a result of the simple and forthright testimony of the woman of Samaria, many of her people believed on the Lord Jesus. All she said was, "He told me all that ever I did," and yet that was sufficient to bring others to the Savior. This should be an encouragement to each of us to be simple, courageous, and direct in our witness for Christ. The reception given to the Lord Jesus by the Samaritans was in marked contrast to that of the Jews. The Samaritans seemed to have some real appreciation of this wonderful Person, and they invited Him to stay with them. As a result, the Lord stayed two days. How privileged this city of Sychar was, that it should entertain the Lord of life and glory during this period of time!

No two conversions are exactly alike. Some believed because of the testimony of the woman (4:41). Many more believed because of the words of the Lord Himself. God uses various means in bringing sinners to Himself. (4:42). It is wonderful to hear these Samaritans bearing such clear testimony to the Savior. There was no doubt in their minds at all. They had complete assurance of salvation based not upon the word of a woman, but upon the words of the Lord Jesus Himself. Having heard Him and believed His words, the Samaritans had come to know that He was indeed the Christ, the Savior of the world. Only the Holy Spirit could have given them this insight. The Jewish people, of course, thought that the Messiah would be for the Jews alone. But the Samaritans realized that the benefits of Christ's mission would extend to all the world.

## The Second Sign: Healing of the Nobleman's Son (4:43-54)

After the two days which He spent among the Samaritans, the Lord Jesus turned His footsteps northward into Galilee.

Verse 44 seems to present a difficulty. It states that the reason for the Savior's moving from Samaria to Galilee was that a prophet has no honor in his own country. And yet Galilee was His own country, since Nazareth was a city located in that region. Perhaps the meaning is that Jesus went into some part of Galilee other than Nazareth. In any case, the statement is true that a person is not usually appreciated as much in his own home town as he is in other places. Certainly the Lord Jesus was not appreciated by His own people as He should have been.

When the Lord returned to Galilee, He was given a favorable reception because the people had seen the things which He had done at the feast in Jerusalem (4:45) Obviously the Galilaeans referred to here were Jews. They had gone down to Jerusalem to worship. There they had seen the Lord and had witnessed some of His mighty works. Now they were willing to have Him in their midst in Galilee, not because they acknowledged Him to be the Son of God, but because they were curiously interested in One who was arousing so much comment everywhere He went.

The village of Cana was honored again by a visit from the Lord (4:46). On the first visit, some there had seen Him turn the water into wine. Now they were to witness another mighty miracle by Him, the effect of which would extend to Capernaum.

The son of a certain nobleman from Capernaum was sick. This man was undoubtedly a Jew employed by Herod, the king. He had heard that Jesus had now returned to Galilee from Judea. He must have had some faith in the ability of Christ to heal because he came directly to Him and pleaded that He would restore his dying son. In this sense, he seems to have had a greater trust in the Lord than most of his fellow countrymen.

Speaking not only to the nobleman, but to the Jewish people in general, the Lord reminded them, in verse 48, of a national characteristic, that they desired to see miracles before they would believe. Generally speaking, Jesus was not as pleased with a faith based on miracles as He was with faith based on His Word alone. It is more honoring to Him to believe a thing simply because He has said it than because He gives some visible proof. It is characteristic of man that he wants to see before he believes. But the Lord Jesus teaches us that we should first believe, and then we will see.

The words "signs" and "wonders" both refer to miracles. "Signs" are miracles that have a deep meaning or significance. "Wonders" are miracles that cause men to be amazed by their supernatural qualities.

The nobleman, with the persistence of faith, believed the Lord Jesus could do his son good, and he wanted a visit from the Lord more than anything else. In one sense, his faith was defective. He thought that the Lord Jesus would have to be at the boy's bedside before He could heal him. However, the Savior did not rebuke him for this but rewarded him for the measure of faith which he did exhibit.

In verse 50 we see the man's faith growing. He exercised what little faith he had, and the Lord gave him more. Jesus sent him home with the promise, "Your son will live." The son had been healed! Without any miracle or visible proof, the man believed the word of the Lord Jesus and started for home. That is faith in action! As the nobleman was nearing home, his servants came out to meet him with the news that his son was well. The man was not at all shocked by this announcement. He had believed the promise of the Lord Jesus, and having believed, he would now see the evidence. He had believed the promise of Jesus but apparently he did not believe the cure would be instantaneous. He inquired of the servants as to the time when his son *began to get better*. Their answer revealed that the healing was not gradual; it had taken place instantly. There could now be not the slightest trace of doubt about this wonderful miracle. At the seventh hour of the previous day, Jesus had said to the nobleman in Cana, "Your son will live." At the very same hour in the village of Capernaum, the son had been healed, and the fever had left him. From this the nobleman learned that it was not necessary for the Lord Jesus to be bodily present in order to work a miracle or answer prayer. This should encourage all Christians in their prayer life. We have a mighty God who hears our requests and who is able to work out His purposes in any part of the world at any time. The nobleman believed and his whole house. It is apparent from this and from similar verses in the New Testament that God loves to see families united in Christ. It is not His will that there should be divided families in heaven. He takes care to record the fact that the whole household believed in His Son.

The healing of the nobleman's son was not the second miracle in the Lord's entire ministry up to this point. It was the second miracle He performed in Galilee after He had come from Judea.

CHAPTER

# 4

# THE IMPOTENT MAN (JOHN 5)

## The Third Sign: Healing of the Impotent Man (5:1-9)

As this chapter opens, we are told that the time had come for one of the Jewish feasts in Jerusalem. Many believe this was the feast of the Passover, but it is impossible to be sure. Born into the world as a Jew, and obedient to the laws that God had made for the Jewish people, the Lord went to Jerusalem for the feast. As Jehovah of the Old Testament, the Lord Jesus had been the One who instituted the Passover in the first place. Now as a Man, obedient to His Father, He obeyed the very laws that He had made.

In the city of Jerusalem, there was a pool named Bethesda. The word "Bethesda" means "house of mercy" or "house of pity." This pool was located by the sheep market, or, as some understand it, by the sheep gate. Around the pool there were five porches or large open spaces capable of holding a number of people. Some Bible teachers think that these five porches represent the Law of Moses and speak of its inability to help man out of his deep troubles.

Apparently the pool of Bethesda was known as a place where miracles of healing occurred (5:3). Whether these miracles took place throughout the year, or only at certain times, such as on feast days, we do not know. Surrounding the pool were a large number of people who had come hoping to be cured. Some were impotent, meaning feeble, weak, or sick; some were blind; others were halt, or lame. Finally, there were those with withered limbs. These various types of infirmity picture sinful man in his helplessness, blindness, lameness, and uselessness. These people, suffering from the effect of sin in their bodies, were waiting for the moving of the water. Their hearts were filled with longing to be freed from their sicknesses, and they earnestly desired to find healing. Someone has said, "They lingered round that uncertain disappointing water, though the Son of God was present. . . . Surely there is a lesson for us in this. The pool thickly populated, and Jesus passing by unheeded! What a witness of man's religion! Ordinances, with all their complicated machinery, sought after, and the grace of God slighted."

The narrative here in verse 4 does not satisfy our curiosity. We are simply told that at a certain time an angel came down and troubled or moved the water. The first one who was able to get into the water at that time was healed of his sickness. You can imagine what a pathetic sight it was to see so many people in need of help, struggling to get into the water, and yet only one being able to receive the healing power. The latter part of verse 3 and all of verse 4 are omitted from many versions of the Bible. (The section beginning with the words "waiting for the moving of the water" and continuing through the end of verse 4 was not a part of the original Gospel of John. Some suggest that the agitation of the water was caused by springs at the bottom of the pool, and that popular opinion attributed the agitation to an angel.)

In verse 5 we discover that one of the men waiting by the pool had been an invalid for thirty-eight years. He had been in this condition even before the Savior was born. The Lord Jesus had complete knowledge of everything. He had never met this man before. Yet He knew that he had been an invalid for a long time. In loving compassion, the Lord asks him in verse 6, "Do you want to be made well?" Jesus knew this was the greatest longing of the man's heart but He wanted to draw out from the man an admission of his own helplessness and of his desperate need for healing. It is the same with salvation. The Lord knows we need to be saved, but He waits to hear the confession from our own lips that we are lost, and need and accept Him as our Savior. We are not saved by our own will, yet the human will must be exercised before God saves a soul.

The answer of the sick man was pathetic. For years he had lain by the pool, waiting to get in, but every time the waters were stirred up, there was no one to help him. Every time he would try to get in, someone always arrived ahead of him. This reminds us how disappointed we are when we depend on our fellow men to save us from our sins. The man's bed was a pad or a light mattress. He was told to rise, to carry this pad, and to walk. When we are saved, we are not only told to rise, but also to walk. The Lord Jesus gives us healing from sin, and then He expects us to walk in a manner that is worthy of Him. The Lord Jesus never tells a person to do a thing without giving him the power to do it. Even as He spoke, new life and power flowed into the body of the invalid. He was healed immediately. It was not a gradual recovery. Limbs that had been useless or weak for years now throbbed with strength. Then there was immediate obedience to the word of the Lord. The man took up his mat and walked. What a thrill it must have been for him to do this after thirty-eight years of sickness!

This miracle took place on the Sabbath. The Sabbath, of course, was the seventh day of the week—our Saturday. The Jewish people were forbidden to do any work on the Sabbath day. This man was a Jew, and yet at the instruction of the Lord Jesus, he did not hesitate to carry his mattress despite Jewish restrictions regarding the day.

## The Opposition of the Jews (5:10-18)

When the Jewish people saw the man carrying his mattress on the Sabbath, they challenged him. For these people were very strict and harsh and cruel in carrying out their religious observances and clung rigidly to the letter of the law, but they themselves did not show mercy and compassion to others. The healed man gave a very simple answer in verse 11. He said that the One who cured him told him to take up his bed and walk. Anyone who had the power to heal a man who had been sick for thirty-eight years ought to be obeyed, even if he instructed a person to carry his bed on the Sabbath! The healed man did not really know who the Lord Jesus was at this time. He spoke of Him in a very general way, and yet with real gratitude.

Naturally the Jews wanted to find out who dared tell this man to break the Sabbath, so they asked him to identify the culprit. The Law of Moses decreed that one who broke the Sabbath should be stoned to death (5:13). The Jews cared little that a paralytic had been healed. The healed man did not know who had cured him. And it was impossible to point Him out, because the Lord had slipped away from the crowd that had gathered.

This incident marks one of the great turning points in the public ministry of the Lord Jesus Christ. Because He performed this miracle on the Sabbath day, He stirred up the anger and hatred of the Jewish people. They began to pursue Him and to seek His life.

Some time later the Lord Jesus found the healed man in the temple where doubtless he was thanking God for the wonderful miracle that had taken place in his life. The Lord reminded him in verse 14 that he had been highly favored and was therefore under solemn obligation. Privilege always brings with it responsibility. "See, you have been made well. Sin no more, lest a worse thing come upon you." The man's sickness had come to him as a result of sin in his life. This is not true of all sickness. Many times illness in a person's life has no direct connection with any sin he has committed. Infants, for instance, may be sick before they are old enough to sin knowingly. "Sin no more," said Jesus, expressing God's standard of holiness. If He had said "sin as little as possible," He would not have been God. God cannot condone sin in any degree. Then the warning was added, "lest a worse thing come upon you." What this "worse thing" might be we are not told. Doubtless the Lord intended the man to understand that sin has far more terrible results than physical sickness. Those who die in their sins are condemned to eternal wrath and anguish.

It is a more serious thing to sin against grace than against law. The Lord Jesus had shown wonderful love and mercy to this man. It would be a poor response to carry on in the same kind of sinful life which had led to his illness.

Like the woman of Samaria, this man desired to bear public witness to his Savior (5:15). He told the Jews that it was Jesus who had made him well again. He wanted to pay tribute to Jesus, though the Jews were not interested in such tribute. Their chief desire was to apprehend Jesus and punish Him.

Here is a terrible exposure of the wicked heart of man. The Savior had come and had performed a great act of healing and these Jews were infuriated. They resented the fact that the miracle took place on the Sabbath. They were cold-blooded religionists, more interested in ceremonial observances than in the blessing and welfare of their fellow men. They did not realize that the very One who originally ordained the Sabbath was the One who now performed an act of mercy on this day. In any case Jesus had not broken the Sabbath. The law forbade menial work on that day, but it did not prohibit the performance of acts of necessity or of mercy.

Having finished the work of creation in six days, God had rested on the seventh day. This was the Sabbath. However, when sin entered into the world, God's rest was disturbed. He would now work ceaselessly to bring men and women back into fellowship with Himself. He would provide a means of redemption. He would send out the gospel message to every generation. Thus, from the time of Adam's fall unto the present time, God has been working ceaselessly, and He is still working. The same was true of the Lord Jesus. He was engaged in His Father's business, and His love and grace could not be confined to only six days of the week.

Verse 18 is very important. It tells us that the Jews became more determined than ever to kill the Lord Jesus. He had not only broken the Sabbath but had claimed equality with God! It seemed quite clear to them that Jesus had broken the Sabbath.

When Jesus spoke of God as His Father, they realized that He was claiming to be equal with God. To them, this was terrible blasphemy. Actually, of course, it was only the truth. The Lord Jesus stated His equality with God in even more positive terms, in the verses that follow. As J. S. Baxter puts it: "He claims equality in seven particulars: (1) Equal in working: 'Whatever He (the Father) does, the Son also does in like manner' (v. 19). (2) Equal in knowing: 'For the Father loves the Son, and shows Him all things that He Himself does' (v. 20). (3) Equal in resurrecting: 'For as the Father raises the dead . . . so the Son gives life to whom He will' (v. 21 with vv. 28, 29). (4) Equal in judging: 'For the Father judges no man, but has committed all judgment to the Son' (v. 22 with v. 27). (5) Equal in honor: 'That all should honour the Son just as they honour the Father' (v. 23). (6) Equal in regenerating: 'He who hears My word and believes in Him who sent Me . . . has passed from death into life' (v. 24). (7) Equal in self-existence: 'For as the Father has life in Himself; so He has granted the Son to have life in Himself' (v. 26)."

## Jesus Defends His Claim to Be Equal with God (5:19-29)

The Lord now claimed to be so closely united with God the Father that He could not act independently. He does not mean that He did not have the power to do anything by Himself, but that He was so closely united with God that He could only do the very things that He saw His Father doing. For while the Lord claimed equality with the Father, He did not claim independency too. He is not independent of the Father though He is fully equal with Him.

The Lord Jesus intended the Jews to think of Him as equal with God. It would be absurd for a mere man to claim to do the very things that God Himself does. The Lord Jesus claims to see what the Father is doing. In order to make such a claim, He must have continual access to the Father and complete knowledge of what is going on in heaven. Not only so, but Jesus claims to do the very things which He sees the Father doing. This is certainly an assertion of His equality with God. He is omnipotent.

It is a special mark of the Father's love for His Son that He shows Him all that He Himself does (5:20). Jesus not only saw these things; He had the power to perform them as well. Then the Savior went on to say that God would show Him greater works than these, so that the people might marvel. Already they had seen the Lord Jesus performing miracles. They had just seen Him healing a man who had been crippled for thirty-eight years. But they would see greater marvels than this. The first such marvel would be the raising of the dead, described in verse 21. The second was the work of judging mankind, spoken of in verse 22.

The Jews accused Jesus of making Himself equal with God. He did not deny the charge, but set forth tremendous proofs of the fact that He and the Father are one. Just as the Father raises the dead and gives life to them, so also the Son gives life to whom He will. Could this ever be said of Him if He were a mere man? To ask the question is to answer it.

According to the New Testament God the Father has committed the work of judgment to His Son. In order for the Lord Jesus to do this work, He must, of course, have absolute knowledge and perfect righteousness. He must be able to discern the thoughts and motives of men's hearts. The Judge of all the earth stood before these Jews, asserting His authority, and yet they did not recognize Him!

Here in verse 23 we have the reason why God has given authority to His Son to raise the dead and to judge the world. All men must honor the Son, even as they honor the Father. This is a most important statement, and one of the clearest proofs in the Bible of the deity of the Lord Jesus Christ. Throughout the Bible we are taught that God alone is to be worshipped. In the Ten Commandments, the people were forbidden to have any god but the one true God. Now we are taught that all men should honor the Son even as they honor the Father. The only conclusion we can come to from this verse is that Jesus Christ is God.

Many people claim to worship God, but deny that Jesus Christ is God. They say He was a good man or more godlike than any other man who ever lived. But this verse puts Him on an absolute equality with God, and requires that men should give Him the same honor which they give to God the Father. If a man does not honor the Son, then he does not honor the Father. It is useless to claim a love for God if one does not have the same love for the Lord Jesus. If you have never realized before who Jesus Christ is, then read this verse carefully, remember that it is the Word of God, and accept the glorious truth that Jesus Christ is God manifest in the flesh.

In the preceding verses, we learned that the Lord Jesus had the power to give life and that, also, the work of judgment had been committed to Him. Now in verse 24 we learn how a man may receive spiritual life from Him and escape judgment.

This is one of the favorite gospel verses in the Bible. Multitudes have become possessors of eternal life through its message. The Lord Jesus began the declaration of this verse with the words "most assuredly," drawing attention to the importance of what He was about to say. Then He added the very personal announcement, "I say to you." The Son of God is speaking to us in a very personal and intimate way.

"He who hears My word." To hear the word of Jesus means not only to listen to it, but also to receive it, to believe it, and to obey it. Many people hear the gospel preached but do nothing about it. The Lord is saying here that a man must accept His teaching as divine, and believe that He is indeed the Savior of the world.

"And believes in Him who sent Me." It is a matter of believing God. This does not mean that a person is saved simply by believing God. Many profess to believe in God, yet they have never been converted. The thought is that one must believe God who sent the Lord Jesus Christ into the world. He must believe that God sent the Lord Jesus to be our Savior. He must believe what God says about the Lord Jesus, namely, that He is the only Savior and that sins can only be put away through His work on Calvary's Cross.

"Has everlasting life." It does not say that he will have eternal life, but that he has it right now. Eternal life is the life of the Lord Jesus Christ. It is not only life that will go on forever, but it is a quality of life, a kind of life. It is the life of the Savior imparted to us who believe on Him. It is the spiritual life received when a man is born again, in contrast to the natural life that he received at his physical birth.

"And shall not come into judgment." The believer is not condemned now and will never be. He is free from condemnation because Christ has paid the penalty for his sins on Calvary's Cross. God will not demand the payment of this penalty twice. Christ has paid it as our Substitute, and that is sufficient. He has finished the work, and nothing can be added to a finished work. The Christian will never be punished for his sins. (There are other verses which teach that a believer will one day stand before the judgment seat of Christ such as Romans 14:10; 2 Corinthians 5:10. However, the question of his sins will not be brought up at that time for punishment. That question was settled at Calvary. At the judgment seat of Christ, the believer's life and service will be reviewed, and he will either receive rewards or suffer loss. It will not be then a question of his soul's salvation, but of his life's fruitfulness.)

"But has passed from death into life." The one who has trusted Christ has passed out of a state of spiritual death into one of spiritual life. Before conversion, he was dead in trespasses and in sins. He was dead as far as love for God or fellowship with the Lord were concerned. When he put his faith in Jesus Christ, he was indwelt by the Spirit of God and became a possessor of divine life.

Here in verse 25 it is the third time that the Lord Jesus has used the expression "most assuredly" in this chapter, and it is the seventh time we have found the words so far in this Gospel. When the Lord said that *the hour* was coming and now is, He was saying that *the time* was coming, and had arrived already. The time referred to was His coming onto the stage of history.

Who are the dead spoken of in this verse? Who is it who would hear the voice of the Son of God and live? This may of course refer to those who were raised from the dead by the Lord during His public ministry. But the verse has a wider meaning than this. The dead are those who are dead in trespasses and in sins. They hear the voice of the Son of God when the gospel is preached. When they accept the message and receive the Savior, then they pass from death unto life.

Verse 26 was added to explain how a person can receive life from the Lord Jesus. Just as the Father is the Source and Giver of life, so He has decreed that the Son, too, should have life in Himself and should be able to give it to others. This is a statement of the deity of Christ and of His equality with the Father. It cannot be said of any man that he has life in himself. Life was given to each one of us, but it was never given to God or to the Lord

Jesus. From all eternity, They have had life dwelling in Them. That life never had a beginning. It never had a source apart from Them.

Furthermore God has given Christ authority to be the Judge of the world. This power to judge has been given to Jesus because He is the Son of man. The Lord is called both Son of God and Son of man. The title *Son of God* reminds us that the Lord Jesus is a Member of the holy Trinity, one of the Persons of the Godhead. As Son of God, He is equal with the Father and with the Holy Ghost, and as Son of God, He gives life. But He is also the *Son of man*. He came into the world as a Man, lived here among men, and died on the Cross of Calvary as a Substitute for men and women. He was rejected and crucified when He came into the world as a Man. When He comes again, He will come to judge His enemies and to be honored in this same world where He was once so cruelly treated. Because He is both God and Man, He is perfectly qualified to be Judge.

Doubtless as Christ was making these strong claims to be equal with God the Father, the Jews who were listening were amazed at His statements (5:28). He realized, of course, the thoughts that were going through their minds, and so He here told them that they should not marvel at these things. Then He went on to reveal to them some even more startling truth. In a time yet future, all of those whose bodies are lying in the grave will hear His voice. How foolish it would be for any one who was not God to predict that bodies lying in the grave would one day hear his voice! Only God could ever support such a statement.

All the dead will one day be raised. Some will be raised to life, and others to condemnation. Every person who has ever lived or will ever live falls into one of these two classes. (If this were the only verse in the Bible on the subject of resurrection, one would think that all the dead will be raised at the same time. However, we know from other portions of Scripture, particularly Revelation 20 that a period of at least one thousand years elapses between the two resurrections. The first resurrection is the resurrection of those who have been saved through faith in Christ. The second resurrection includes all who have died as unbelievers).

Verse 29 does not teach that people who have done good will be saved because of their good deeds, and those who have done evil will be condemned because of their wicked lives. A person is not saved by doing good, but he does good because he has been saved. Good works are not the root of salvation but rather the fruit. They are not the cause, but the effect. The expression "they that have done evil" describes those who have never put their faith and trust in the Lord Jesus, and consequently whose lives have been evil in the sight of God. These will be raised to stand before God and to be sentenced to eternal doom.

## Four Witnesses to Jesus as the Son of God (5:30-47)

The thought of verse 30 is that the Lord is so closely united with God the Father that He could not act by Himself. He could not do anything on His own authority. There was no trace of willfulness in the Savior. He acted in perfect obedience to His Father and always in fullest fellowship and harmony with Him.

This verse has often been used by false teachers to support their claim that Jesus Christ was not God. They say that because He could not do anything of His own self, therefore He was just a man. But the verse proves the very opposite. Men can do the things they want, whether they are in accordance with the will of God or not. But because of who He was, the Lord Jesus could not so act. It was not a physical impossibility, but a moral impossibility. He had the physical power to do all things, but He could not do anything that was wrong: and it would have been wrong for Him to have done anything that was not the will of God the Father for Him. This statement sets the Lord Jesus apart from every other man who ever lived.

As the Lord Jesus listened to His Father and daily received instructions from His Father, so He thought, and taught, and acted. The word "judge" in this verse does not here have the sense of deciding on legal matters but rather of deciding what was proper for Him to do and to say. Because the Savior had no selfish motives, He could decide matters fairly and impartially. His one ambition was to please His Father and to do His will. Nothing was allowed to stand in the way of this. Therefore, His judgment of matters was not influenced by what would be for His own best advantage. Our opinions and teachings are affected by what we want to do and what we want to believe. But it was not so with the Son of God. His opinions or judgments were not biased in His own favor. He was without prejudice.

In the remaining verses of this chapter, the Lord Jesus Christ described the various witnesses to His deity. There was the witness of John the Baptist (vv. 32-35); the witness of His works (v. 36); the witness of the Father (vv. 37-38); and the witness of the Old Testament Scriptures (vv. 39-47).

First Jesus made a general statement on the subject of witnessing. He said, "If I bear witness of Myself, My witness is not true." The witness of a single person was not considered sufficient evidence in a court of law. God's divine decree was that two or three witnesses were required to establish testimony, and to make it possible for a valid judgment to be formed. And so the Lord Jesus was about to give not two or three, but four witnesses to His deity.

There is a question as to whether verse 32 refers to John the Baptist, to God the Father, or to the Holy Spirit. Some believe that the word "another" describes John the Baptist and that this verse is linked with the three that follow. Others believe that the Lord here was speaking about the witness that the Holy Spirit bears concerning Him. We believe that He was referring to the witness of the Father.

Having introduced the greatest of all witnesses, His Father, the Lord then turned to *the testimony of John.* He reminded the unbelieving Jews in verse 33 that they sent men to John to hear what he had to say, and John's testimony was all about Him. Instead of pointing men to himself, he pointed them to the Savior. He bore witness to the One who is the truth.

The Lord Jesus reminded His listeners in verse 34 that His claim to be equal with God was not based simply on the testimony of human beings. If that was all He had, then His case would indeed be a weak one. However, He introduced the testimony of John the Baptist since he was a man sent from God and since he testified that the Lord Jesus was indeed the Messiah, the Lamb of God who takes away the sin of the world.

Then He added, "But I say these things that you may be saved." Why was the Lord Jesus speaking to the Jews at such great length? Was He simply trying to show that He was right and that they were wrong? On the contrary, He was bringing before them these wonderful truths in order that they might realize who He was and accept Him as the promised Savior. This verse gives us a wonderful view of the loving and tender heart of the Lord Jesus. He spoke to those who hated Him and who would soon be seeking in every possible way to take His life. But there was no hatred in His heart toward them. He could only love them.

Here in verse 35 the Lord pays tribute to John the Baptist as "the burning and shining lamp." This meant that he was a very zealous man, one who had a ministry that brought light to others, and one who was consumed in the process of pointing people to Jesus. At first, the Jewish people had flocked to John the Baptist. He was something of a novelty, a strange figure who had come into their lives, and they went out to listen to him. For a season, they accepted him as a popular religious teacher. They rejoiced temporarily, but there was no repentance. Why then, after accepting John so warmly, would they not accept the One of whom John preached? They were inconsistent. They received the forerunner, but would not receive the King. Jesus paid high tribute to John. For any servant of Christ to be called a burning and shining lamp is true praise from the Son of God. May each of us who loves the Lord Jesus desire that we, too, may be flames of fire for Him, burning ourselves out as we bring light to the world.

The testimony of John was not Christ's greatest proof of His deity (5:36). The *miracles* which the Father gave Him to do bore witness of Him, that He had been truly sent by God the Father. Miracles in themselves are not a proof of deity. In the Bible, we read of men who were given the power to perform miracles, and we even read of evil beings with the power to do supernatural wonders. But the miracles of the Lord Jesus were different from all others. He had the power *in Himself* to do these mighty works, whereas others were given the power. Other men have performed miracles, but they could not confer the power to perform miracles on others. The Lord Jesus not only performed miracles Himself, but He gave His apostles the authority to do likewise. The mighty works performed by the Savior moreover were the very ones prophesied in the Old Testament concerning the Messiah. Finally, the miracles that the Lord Jesus performed were unique in character, scope and number.

Again the Lord spoke of the witness which *the Father* had borne to Him (5:37). Perhaps this referred to the time when the Lord Jesus was baptized. Then the voice of God the Father was heard from heaven stating that Jesus was His beloved Son, in whom He was well pleased. But it should be added that in the life and ministry and miracles of the Lord Jesus, the Father also bore witness to the fact that He was the very Son of God.

The unbelieving Jews had neither heard the voice of God at any time nor seen His form. They had not heard God's voice at any time because they did not have His word abiding in them. God speaks to men through the Bible. These Jews had the Old Testament Scriptures, but they did not allow God to speak to them through the Scriptures. Their hearts were hardened, and their ears were dull of hearing.

They had never seen God's form or person because they did not believe on the One whom God had sent. God the Father does not have a form or shape that is visible to mortal eyes. He is Spirit and therefore invisible. But God has revealed Himself to men in the Person of the Lord Jesus Christ. Those who believed on Christ in a very real way saw the form of God. Unbelievers merely looked upon Him as another man like themselves.

*The Scriptures* were a witness to Christ. The first part of verse 39 may be understood in two ways. The Lord Jesus may by telling the Jews to search the Scriptures. Or He may be simply stating the fact that they did search the Scriptures because they thought that in the mere possession of the Scriptures, they had eternal life. Either interpretation of the verse is possible. Probably the Lord Jesus was simply stating the fact that the Jews searched the Scriptures and thought that in doing so they were receiving eternal life. They did not realize that the Old Testament Scriptures telling of the coming Messiah were actually telling about Jesus. It is terrible to think that men with the Scriptures in their hands could be so blind. But it was even more inexcusable that after the Lord Jesus spoke to them in this way, they still refused to accept Him. Notice the latter part of this verse carefully. "They are they which testify of me." This simply means that the main subject of the Old Testament Scriptures was the coming of Christ. If anyone misses that in studying the Old Testament, he misses the most important part of it.

The Jews were not willing to come to Christ that they might have life. Here we have the real reason why men do not accept the Savior. It is not because they cannot understand the gospel, or find it impossible to believe on Jesus. There is nothing about the Lord Jesus that makes it impossible for them to trust Him. The real fault lies in man's own will. He loves his sins more than he loves the Savior. He does not want to give up his wicked ways.

In condemning the Jews for their failure to receive Him, the Lord did not want them to think that He was hurt because they had not given Him honor (5:41). He did not come into the world for the purpose of being praised by the men of this world. He was not dependent on their praise, but rather sought the praise of His Father. Even if men rejected Him, that did not detract from His glory.

Man's failure to receive the Son of God is traced back to its cause. These men did not have the love of God in them, that is, they loved themselves rather than God. If they had loved God, they would have received the One whom God had sent. By their rejection of the Lord Jesus, they showed their utter lack of love for Jehovah.

The Lord Jesus came in His Father's Name, that is, He came to do His Father's will, to bring glory to His Father, and to obey His Father in all things. If men had really loved God, they would have loved the One who sought to please God in all that He did and said.

The Lord predicted in verse 44 that another man would come in his own name and that the Jews would receive him. Perhaps in one sense He was referring to many false teachers who arose after Him and sought to be honored by the nation. Perhaps He was referring to leaders of false cults down through the centuries who have claimed to be the Christ. But more probably He was referring here to the antichrist. In a coming day, a self-appointed ruler will rise among the Jewish people and demand to be worshipped as God (2 Thessalonians 2:8-10). The majority of the Jewish nation will accept this antichrist as their ruler, and as a result they will come under severe judgment from God (Revelation 13:11-18; Matthew 24:15).

Then the Lord gave another reason for the failure of the Jewish people to accept Him. They were more interested in the approval of their fellow men than they were in God's approval. They were not willing to endure the reproach and suffering which would be heaped upon them if they became followers of Him. As long as a man is afraid of what others will say or do, he cannot be saved. In order to believe on the Lord Jesus, one must desire God's approval more than anyone else's. He must seek the honor that comes from the only God.

The Lord would not need to accuse these Jews to the Father. There were many charges He could bring against them, but there would be no need for Him to do so because the writings of Moses would be sufficient to accuse them (5:45). The Jews took great pride in the Old Testament Scriptures and especially in the writings of Moses. They were proud that these Scriptures were given to the Jewish nation, but they did not obey the words of Moses, as we shall see in the next verse.

The Lord Jesus put the writings of Moses on the same level of authority as His own words. "All scripture is given by inspiration of God." Whether we read the Old Testament or the New Testament, we are reading the Word of God. If the Jews had believed Moses, they would have believed the Lord Jesus also because Moses wrote concerning the coming of Christ. In Deuteronomy 18:15, 18, Moses predicted the coming of Christ, and told the Jewish people to listen to Him and obey Him when He came. Now the lord Jesus had come, but the Jews failed to receive Him. Thus He said that Moses would accuse them to the Father because they pretended to believe in Moses and yet they did not do what Moses commanded. The words "he wrote of me" are a clear statement by our Lord that the Old Testament Scriptures contain prophecies about Him.

If the Jews would not believe the writings of Moses, it was not likely that they would believe the sayings of Jesus (5:47). There is a close connection between the Old Testament and the New. If a man doubts the inspiration of the Old Testament Scriptures, it is not likely that he will accept the words of the Lord Jesus as being inspired. If men attack certain portions of the Bible, it will not be long before they cast doubt on the rest of the Book as well.

CHAPTER

# 5

# Bread from Heaven (John 6)

## The Fourth Sign: Feeding of the Five Thousand (6:1-15)

The expression "after these things" in verse 1 of chapter 6 means that a period of time had elapsed since the events recorded in chapter 5 took place. Just how much time had passed we do not know. But we do know that Jesus had traveled from the area around Jerusalem up to the Sea of Galilee. When it says that He crossed the sea, it probably means that He went from the northwestern shore to the northeastern side. The Sea of Galilee was also known as the sea of Tiberias, doubtless because the city of Tiberias was located on its western bank. This city was the capital of the province of Galilee and was named after the Roman Emperor Tiberius. A great crowd of people followed after Him, not necessarily because they believed on Him as the Son of God, but because they saw His miracles. There was a prominent mountain in that area, and the Lord Jesus went up there with His disciples. (The translation of this verse should be "and Jesus went up into *the* mountain.")

It is not clear why John mentioned in verse 4 that the Passover was about to be held. Some suggest that the Lord Jesus was probably thinking about the Passover when He gave His wonderful message in this chapter on the true Bread of Life. The Lord Jesus had not gone to Jerusalem for this Passover. John spoke of the Passover as "a feast of the Jews." Actually, it had been instituted by God and had been given to the Jewish people, and in that sense it was a feast of the Jews. But the expression might also mean that God no longer recognized it as "a feast of Jehovah" because the Jewish nation celebrated it as a mere ritual, without any real heart interest.

Jesus was not annoyed when He saw the multitude, thinking they would disturb His rest or His time with the disciples. His first thought was to provide something for them to eat (6:5). So He turned to Philip and asked where bread could be purchased to feed the multitude. When Jesus asked a question, it was never to add to His own knowledge, but to teach others. He knew the answer, but Philip didn't. The Lord was going to teach Philip a valuable lesson and to test his faith. Jesus knew He would perform a miracle to feed this great crowd of people. But did Philip realize He was able to do this? Was Philip's faith great or was it small?

From verse seven we see that Philip's faith did not rise to very great heights. He made a rapid estimate and decided two hundred pennies' worth of bread would not be enough to provide even a little meal for everyone. We do not know exactly how much bread could be purchased for that amount but it must have been plenty. A penny was a working man's daily wage.

Andrew, Simon Peter's brother, was present. They both lived in the general vicinity of Bethsaida, along the shore of the Sea of Galilee. Andrew also decided it would be difficult to feed such a throng. However, he noticed a boy with five barley loaves and two small fishes, but he felt that these would be almost useless in attempting to satisfy the hunger of so many people. This little boy did not have much, but he was willing to put it at the disposal of the Lord Jesus. As a result, this story is recorded in each of the four Gospels. He did not do much, but "little is much if God is in it," and he has become famous throughout the world.

The first time the word "men" is used in verse 10, it means mankind in general and includes both male and female. The second time it is used, it means men in contrast to women. In making the people sit down (or recline), the Lord Jesus provided for their comfort. Notice He chose a place where there was much grass. It was unusual to find such a place in that region, but the Lord took care that the crowd would be seated in a clean, pleasant place.

There were five thousand men in the crowd which means there were many women and children in addition. Five thousand are mentioned to indicate what a mighty miracle was about to take place.

There is a lesson for us in verse 11 when Jesus took the five loaves and gave thanks for them. If Jesus did this before partaking of food or serving it, how much more should we thank God before eating our meals. Next He distributed the food to the disciples.

The Lord did not do everything Himself. He enlisted the service of others. It has been well said, "You do what you can do; I'll do what I can do; and the Lord will do what we cannot do."

By the time the Lord distributed the bread to the disciples, it had been wonderfully multiplied. We don't know the exact moment when this miracle took place, but we do know that those five loaves and two small fishes became enough in the Lord's hands to feed this great throng. The disciples served the bread and the fishes to those who were seated. There was no scarcity because they gave them of the fishes "as much as they wanted." This miracle involved a true act of creation. No mere man could take five loaves and two small fishes and multiply them in such a way as this. It has been well said, "'Twas springtime when He blessed the bread, 'twas harvest when He brake."

Verse 12 provides a very beautiful touch. If Jesus had been a mere man, He would never have bothered to think about the remaining fragments. Any man who can feed five thousand does not worry about the few crumbs that are left over. But Jesus is God, and with God there must be no wasting of His bounties. He does not want us to squander the precious things He has given to us, and so He instructs that the broken pieces be gathered up that nothing might be lost.

Many people try to explain away this miracle. The crowd, they say, saw the boy give his loaves and fishes to Jesus. This made others realize how selfish they were, so they took out their lunches and shared with each other. In this way, there was plenty of food for everyone. But twelve baskets of bread were gathered up after the people had finished eating. But could this be if each person had his own lunch or shared someone else's? No, indeed! On the contrary, a mighty miracle had been performed!

We see in verse 14 that the people themselves recognized the miracle. They were so convinced it was a miracle that they acknowledged Jesus to be the Prophet who would come into the world. They knew a prophet was coming, and looked for him to deliver them from the might of Rome. But they were not willing to admit that Jesus was the Son of God. Neither were they willing to confess their sins and to accept Him as Savior. As a result of

Jesus' miracle, the people wanted to make Him King. But Jesus was not moved by their carnal wishes. He had come into the world to die as a Substitute for sinners on the Cross of Calvary. He would do nothing to interfere with that object. He must suffer, bleed, and die before being exalted.

## The Fifth Sign: Jesus Walks on Water and Rescues His Disciples (6:16-21)

It was now evening. Jesus had gone into the mountain alone. The crowd had been sent home, and the disciples went down to the beach to prepare for their trip back across the Sea of Galilee. As they went over the sea toward Capernaum, it was dark. The Lord was not with them. He was up on the mountain praying. What a picture of Christ's followers today! They are on the stormy sea of life. It is dark. The Lord Jesus is nowhere to be seen. But that does not mean that He is unaware of what is going on. He is in heaven praying for those He loves.

The Sea of Galilee is subject to very violent storms. Winds sweep down the valley of the Jordan River and raise mountainous waves on the Sea of Galilee. It is not safe for small boats to be out on the sea at such a time. The disciples had rowed about twenty-five or thirty furlongs (between three and four miles) and were in great danger from just such a storm. Suddenly they looked up and saw Jesus walking on the water, and coming near to them and they were afraid.

Notice how simply the story is told. The most amazing facts are being told to us, but John did not use big words to impress us with the greatness of what was taking place. Instead he used great restraint in setting forth the facts.

The Lord Jesus spoke a wonderful word of comfort in verse 20. "It is I; be not afraid," He said. The mighty Creator, the Sustainer of the universe, was at hand. There was no reason to fear. He who made the Sea of Galilee could cause its waters to be calm and could bring His disciples safely to shore. The words "It is I" were literally "I AM." So for the second time in John's Gospel Jesus appropriated to Himself the name of Jehovah. When they realized it was the Lord, the disciples welcomed Him aboard. As soon as they did this, they found themselves at their destination. Here another miracle is stated but not explained. They did not have to row any farther. The Lord Jesus brought them to dry land instantly. What a wonderful Person He is!

## The People Seek a Sign (6:22-34)

It is now the next day. Multitudes are still in the area northeast of the Sea of Galilee. They had watched the disciples get into the small boat the previous evening and they knew that the Lord Jesus had not gone with them. Only one boat had been available at that time, and the disciples had taken it.

The following day, additional small boats came from Tiberias to the place where the Lord Jesus had fed the multitude. But the Lord could not have departed in one of these because they had just arrived. Perhaps it was in these small boats that the multitude crossed over to Capernaum, as recorded in verses 24 and 25.

The crowd had watched the Lord Jesus very carefully. They knew that He had gone up into the mountain to pray. They knew that He had not gone in the boat with the disciples across the lake. Yet on the following day He was nowhere to be found. They decided to cross the sea to Capernaum, where the disciples were most likely to be. They could not understand how Jesus could be there, but they went in search of Him anyway. Arriving at Capernaum, they found him there. They could not conceal their curiosity, and asked Him how he had arrived. The Lord did not answer their question directly. He realized they did not seek Him because of who He was but because of the food which He gave them. They had seen him perform a mighty miracle on the day before. This should have convinced them that He was indeed the Creator and the Messiah. But their interest was simply in food. They had eaten of the miracle loaves, and their hunger had been satisfied. So Jesus, in verse 27, first advised them not to labor for the meat (i.e., food) which perishes. The Lord did not mean that they should not work for their daily living, but He did mean that this should not be the supreme air of their lives. The satisfaction of hunger is not the most important thing in life. Man consists not only of body, but of spirit, soul, and body. We should labor for the food which endures unto everlasting life, which is the spiritual food or teaching of the Lord Jesus. The value of physical food ends at the grave, the value of the words of the Lord Jesus never ends. It endures unto everlasting life. Man should not live as if his body and its needs were everything. He should make sure that his soul is fed day by day with the Word of God. "Man shall not live bread alone, but by every word that proceeds out of the mouth of God." We should work tirelessly to acquire a better knowledge of the Word of God.

When the Lord Jesus said, in the latter part of the verse, that God the Father had sealed Him, He meant that God had sent Him and approved Him. When we set our seal to something, it means that we promise that it is true. God sealed the Son of man in the sense that He endorsed Him as One who spoke the truth.

The people now asked the Lord what they must do to work the works of God (6:28). Man is always trying to earn his way to heaven. He likes to feel that there is something he can do to merit salvation. Jesus saw through their hypocrisy. They pretended that they wanted to work for God, yet wanted nothing to do with the Son. Jesus told them they must first accept the One whom God had sent. So it is today. Many are seeking to earn their way to heaven by good works. But before they can do good works for God, they must first believe on the Lord Jesus Christ. Good works do not precede salvation, they follow it. The only good work a sinner can do is to confess his sins and receive Jesus Christ as his Lord and Savior.

We learn from verse 30 how wicked were the hearts of the people! Just yesterday they had seen the Lord feed five thousand men with five loaves and two fishes. Today they ask Him for some miracle that would prove His claims to be the Son of God. Going back to the Old Testament, the Jews reminded the Lord Jesus of the miracle of the manna in the wilderness. Their implication was that Jesus had done nothing as wonderful as that. They quoted from Psalm 78:24-25, where it is written, "He gave them bread from heaven to eat." The inference was that Moses called down food from heaven; the Lord was not as great as Moses, because He had only multiplied existing food. (The manna was a small, round, white food which God miraculously provided for Israel in the wilderness. They had to gather the manna from the ground each morning of the first six days of every week).

In verse 32 Jesus replied that it was not Moses who gave them the manna, but it was God who provided it. Moreover, the manna was not the true spiritual bread from heaven. The manna was literal food, designed for the physical body, but it had no value beyond this life. The Lord Jesus was here speaking about the true, ideal, and genuine bread which God gives out of heaven. It is bread for the soul and not for the body. The words "my Father" were a claim by Christ to deity.

The Lord Jesus did not at this point claim to be the bread of God. He simply said the bread of God was that bread which came down out of heaven and which was life-giving. He was showing the superiority of the bread of God to the manna in the wilderness. The manna did not give life but only sustained physical life. It was not intended for the whole world but only for the nation of Israel. The true bread which comes from heaven imparts life to men, and not just to one nation but to all the world. The Jews still did not realize that the Lord Jesus was speaking about Himself as the true bread, and so they asked Him for the bread. They were still thinking in terms of literal bread and there was no real faith in their hearts.

## "I am the Bread of Life" (6:35-65)

Now the Lord Jesus in verse 35 stated the truth simply and clearly. He is the Bread of Life. Those who come to Him find enough in Him to satisfy their spiritual hunger forever. Those who believe on Him find their thirst forever quenched. You will notice the words "I am" in this verse and recognize the Lord was making a claim to equality with Jehovah. It would be folly for a sinful man to utter such words as these. No mere man can satisfy his own spiritual hunger or thirst, to say nothing of satisfying the spiritual appetite of the whole world.

We saw in verse 30 that the unbelieving Jews had asked the Lord for a sign so they might see and believe. Here Jesus said He had already told them that they had seen *Him*—the greater sign of all—and yet they did not believe. If the Son of God could stand before them in perfect manhood and not be recognized by them, then it was doubtful that any sign would convince them.

The Lord was not discouraged by the unbelief of the Jews. He knew that all the Father's purpose and plans would be fulfilled. Even if the Jews to whom He was speaking would not accept Him, all those chosen by God would come to Him. As Pink puts it, "The realization of the invincibility of the eternal counsels of God gives a calmness, a poise, a courage, a perseverance which nothing else can."

Verse 37 is very important because it teaches two of the most important truths in the Bible. First, God has given certain ones to Christ and all those whom He has given will be saved. Second, man is a responsible creature. To be saved, a man must come to the Lord Jesus and accept Him by faith. God does choose some men to be saved, but He does not choose some to be damned. If anyone is saved, it is because of the free grace of God. But if anyone perishes forever, it is his own fault. All men are condemned by their own sinfulness and wickedness. If all men went to hell, they would be receiving only what they deserve. In grace, God stoops down and saves individual people out of the great mass of humanity. Does He have the right to do this? He certainly does. God can do whatever He wants to do and no man can deny Him this right. Moreover, God cannot do anything wrong, unjust, or unfair.

God has elected certain persons to salvation but man is responsible to accept the gospel. God makes a universal offer that if a person will believe on the Lord Jesus Christ, he will be saved. God does not save men against their will. A man must come to Him in repentance and in faith. Then God will save him. No one who comes to God through Christ will be cast out. The human mind cannot reconcile these two teachings. However, we should believe them even if we cannot understand them. They are Biblical teachings and are clearly stated in this verse.

In the verse 37, the Lord Jesus had said that all God's plans would eventually be fulfilled with regard to the salvation of those who were given to Him. Since this was the Father's will, the Lord Jesus would personally undertake to bring it to pass, as His mission was to do the will of God. In verse 38 Jesus adds more information. "I have come down from heaven," said Christ, clearly teaching that His life did not begin in the manger at Bethlehem. Rather, He existed from all eternity with God the Father in heaven. Coming into the world, He was the obedient Son of God. He voluntarily took the place of a servant in order to carry out the will of His Father. This does not mean He did not have a will of His own, but rather that His will was in perfect agreement with the will of God.

The will of the Father was that everyone who was given to Christ would be saved and kept until the resurrection of the just, when they would be raised and taken home to heaven (6:37). The words "nothing" and "it" refer to believers but not to individual believers. They refer to the entire body of Christians who would be saved down through the years. The Lord Jesus was responsible to see that not one member of the body would be lost but that the whole body would be raised up at the last day. "The last day," as far as *Christians* are concerned, refers to the day when the Lord Jesus will come in the air and when believers will be caught up to meet Him and to be forever with Him. To the *Jews,* it meant the coming of the Messiah in glory.

The Lord now went on in verse 40 to explain how a person becomes a member of the family of the redeemed. God's will is that everyone who sees the Son and believes on Him should have everlasting life. To "see the

Son" does not mean to see Him with the physical eye but with the eye of faith. One must see or recognize that Jesus Christ is the Son of God and the Savior of the world. Then, too, he must believe on Him. By a definite act of faith, he must receive the Lord Jesus as his own Lord and Savior. All who do this receive everlasting life as a present possession and also receive the assurance that they will be raised at the last day.

The people were quite unprepared to accept the Lord Jesus, and they showed this by murmuring against Him. He had claimed to be the Bread of God come down from heaven. They realized that this was a claim of great importance. To come down from heaven, one could not be a mere man or even a great prophet. And so the murmured at Him because they were not willing to believe His words. They assumed that Jesus was the son of Joseph. Of course, they were wrong. Jesus was born of the Virgin Mary and conceived of the Holy Ghost. Joseph was not His father. Their failure to believe in the virgin birth led to their darkness and unbelief. So it is today. Those who refuse to accept the Lord Jesus as the Son of God who came into the world through the womb of the virgin find themselves compelled to deny all the great truths concerning the Person and work of Christ.

They had not been speaking directly to Jesus, but we know from verse 43 that He knew what they were saying, and told them not to murmur among themselves. The following verses explain why their murmuring was useless and profitless. The more the Jews rejected the testimony of the Lord Jesus, the more difficult His teachings became. "Light rejected is light denied." The more they spurned the gospel, the harder it became for them to accept the gospel. If the Lord Jesus told them simple things and they would not believe, then He would expound to them more difficult things and they would be thoroughly ignorant of what He was saying.

Man in himself is utterly hopeless and helpless. He does not even have the strength to come to Jesus by himself (6:44). Unless the Father first begins to work in his heart and life, he will never realize his terrible guilt and his need of a Savior. Many people have difficulty with this verse. They suppose it teaches that a man may desire to be saved and yet might find it impossible. This is not so. The verse teaches in the strongest possible way that God is the One who first acts in our lives and seeks to win us to Himself. We have the choice of accepting the Lord Jesus or refusing Him. But we would never have had the desire in the first place if God had not spoken to our hearts. Again the Lord added the promise that He will raise up every true believer at the last day. As we have seen before, this refers to the coming of Christ for His saints, when the dead will be raised and the living will be changed. It is a resurrection of believers only.

Having stated in strong terms that no man could come to Him unless the Father drew him, the Lord goes on in verse 45 to explain how the Father draws men. First, He quotes from Isaiah 54:13. "And they shall all be taught of God." God not only simply chooses certain individuals, He does something about it. He speaks to the hearts of men through the teaching of His precious Word. Then man's own will is involved. Those who respond to the teaching of God's Word and who learn of the Father are the ones who come to Christ. Here again the two great truths of God's sovereignty and man's free will are placed side by side. They show that salvation has a divine side and a human side. When the Lord Jesus said, "It is written in the prophets," He meant, of course, the books of the prophets. He meant Isaiah in particular, but the thought He here expressed is found throughout all the prophets. It is by the teaching of God's Word and God's Spirit that men are drawn to God.

The fact that men are taught of God does not mean that they have seen Him. The only One who has seen the Father is the One who came from God, even the Lord Jesus Himself. All those who are taught of God are taught about the Lord Jesus Christ because God's teaching has Christ Himself as its grand Subject.

One of the clearest and briefest statements in all the Word of God concerning the way of salvation is found in verse 47. The Lord Jesus stated in words that could hardly be misunderstood that whoever believes on Him has everlasting life. Notice He introduced these words with His familiar "most assuredly." This is one of many verses in the New Testament which teaches that salvation is not by works, not by law-keeping, not by church membership, not by obeying the Golden Rule, but simply by believing in the Lord Jesus Christ.

The Lord Jesus states in verse 48 that *He* is the Bread of Life of which He had been speaking. The "bread of life" means, of course, the bread which gives life to those who eat of it. The Jews had previously brought up the subject of the manna in the wilderness and challenged the Lord Jesus to produce some food as wonderful as that. The Lord reminded them that their fathers had eaten the manna and were dead. In other words, the manna was for this life only. It did not have any power to give everlasting life to those who ate it. By the expression, "Your fathers," the Lord dissociated Himself from fallen humanity and implied His unique deity.

In contrast to the manna, the Lord Jesus spoke of Himself, in verse 50, as the Bread which cometh down from heaven. If any man ate of this Bread, he would not die. This did not mean that he would not die physically, but that he would have everlasting life in heaven. Even if he did die physically, his body would be raised at the last day, and he would spend eternity with the Lord.

In this and in the following verses, the Lord Jesus spoke repeatedly of men eating of Him. What does He mean by this? Does He mean that men must eat of Him in a physical, literal way? Obviously, that idea is impossible and repulsive. Some think, however, that we must eat of Him in the communion service; that in some miraculous way the bread and wine are changed into the body and blood of Christ and that in order to be saved we must partake of those emblems. But this is not what Jesus said. The context makes it quite clear that to "eat of Him" means to believe on Him. When we trust the Lord Jesus Christ as our Savior, we appropriate Him by faith. We partake of the benefits of His Person and of His work.

Jesus is the living Bread. He not only lives in Himself, but is life-giving. Those who eat of this Bread will live forever. But how can this be? How can the Lord give eternal life to guilty sinners? The answer is found in the latter part of this verse. "The bread that I will give is my flesh, which I will give for the life of the world." Here the Lord Jesus was pointing forward to His death on the Cross. He would give His life as a ransom for sinners. His body would be broken, and His blood would be poured out as a sacrifice for sins. He would die as a Substitute. He would pay the penalty our sins demanded. And why would He do this? "For the life of the world." He would not die just for the Jewish nation, or even just for the elect. His death would be sufficient for the whole world. This does not mean of course that the whole world will be saved, but that the work of the Lord Jesus at Calvary would be sufficient in its value to save the whole world, if all men came to Jesus.

The Jews were still thinking in terms of literal, physical bread and flesh (6:52). Their thoughts were unable to rise above the things of this life. They did not realize that the Lord Jesus was using physical things to teach spiritual truths. And so they asked among themselves how a mere man could possibly give his flesh to be eaten by others. Once again the Lord Jesus, knowing all things, knew exactly what they were thinking and saying. He warned them solemnly that if they did not eat His flesh and drink His blood, they would have no life in them. This could not refer to the bread and the wine which were used at the Lord's Supper. When the Lord Jesus instituted His Supper, on the night in which He was betrayed, His body had not yet been broken and His blood had not yet been shed. The disciples partook of the bread and the wine, but they did not literally eat His flesh and drink His blood. The Lord Jesus was simply stating that unless we appropriate to ourselves by faith the value of His death for us on Calvary's Cross, we can never be saved. We must believe on Him, we must receive Him, we must trust Him, and we must make Him our very own.

Compare verse 54 with verse 47. It proves that to eat His flesh and to drink His blood means to believe on Him. In verse 47, we read that "he who *believes* in me has everlasting life." In verse 54, we learn that those who *eat* His flesh and *drink* His blood have eternal life. Now things equal to the same thing are equal to each other. To eat His flesh and to drink His blood is to believe on Him. All who believe on Him will be raised up at the last day. This refers, of course, to the bodies of those who have died trusting in the Lord Jesus.

The flesh of the Lord Jesus is true food, and His blood is true drink. This is in contrast to the food and drink of this world which is only of temporary value. The value of the death of the Lord Jesus is never-ending. Those who partake of Him by faith receive life that goes on eternally. A very close union exists between Himself and those who are believers in Him. Those who eat His flesh and drink His blood dwell in Him, and He dwells in them. Nothing could be closer or more intimate than this. When we eat literal food, we take it into our very being; and it becomes a part of us. When we accept the Lord Jesus as our Redeemer, He comes into our lives to dwell, and we, too, dwell in Him.

In verse 57 the Lord Jesus gave another illustration of the close bond that existed between Himself and His people. The illustration was His own connection with God the Father. The living Father had sent the Lord Jesus into the world. (The expression "living Father" means the Father who is the Source of life.) As a Man here in the world, the Lord Jesus lived by the Father, that is, because of the Father or by reason of the Father. His life was lived in closest union and harmony with God the Father. God was the center and circumference of His life. His purpose was to be occupied with God the Father. He was here as a Man in the world, and the world did not realize that He was God manifest in the flesh. Although He was misunderstood by the world, yet He and His Father were one. They lived in closest intimacy. That is exactly the way it is with those who are believers in the Lord Jesus. They are here in the world, misunderstood by the world, and hated and persecuted. But because they have put their faith and trust in the Lord Jesus, they live by reason of Him. Their lives are closely bound up with His life, and this life shall endure forever.

Verse 58 seems to be a summary of all that the Lord has said in the previous verses. He is the Bread which came down from heaven. He is superior to the manna which the fathers ate in the wilderness. That bread was only of temporary value. It was only for this life. But Christ is the Bread of God who gives eternal life to all who eat of Him.

You will remember that the crowd had followed the Lord Jesus and His disciples to Capernaum from the northeast side of the lake. Apparently the multitude had found Jesus in the synagogue, and it was there that He delivered the message on the Bread of Life to them. (A synagogue is a Jewish religious meeting place, but is not the same as the temple, where the sacrifices were offered.)

By this time, the Lord Jesus had many disciples, in addition to the original twelve. Anyone who followed Him and professed to accept His teachings was known as a disciple. However, not all those who were known as His disciples were real believers. Now some of those who professed to be His disciples said, "This is an hard saying." They meant that His teaching was offensive. It was not so much that it was hard for them to understand it, as that it was distasteful for them to receive it. They said, "Who can hear it?" meaning, "Who can stand and listen to such offensive doctrine?"

Here again in verse 61 we find evidence that Jesus was possessed with complete knowledge. He knew exactly what the disciples were saying, that they were murmuring at His claim to have come down from heaven and that they did not like it when He said that men must eat His flesh and drink His blood to have everlasting life. And so He asked them, "Does this offend you?"

They took offense because He said that He had come down from heaven. Now He asked them what they would think if they should see Him ascend back into heaven, which He knew He would do after His resurrection. Also, they were offended by His saying that men must eat His flesh. What would they think, then, if they should see that body of flesh ascend back to heaven? How would men be able to eat His literal flesh and drink His literal blood after He had gone back to the Father?

These men had been thinking in terms of Christ's literal flesh, but in verse 63 He told them that eternal life was not gained by eating flesh but by the work of the Holy Spirit of God. Flesh cannot give life; only the Spirit can do this. They had taken His words in a literal manner and had not realized that they were to be understood spiritually. The Lord Jesus explained that the words that He had spoken were spirit and life; that is when His saying about eating His flesh and drinking His blood are understood in a spiritual way, as meaning belief in Him, then those who accept the message receive eternal life.

Even as He said these things, the Lord realized that some of His listeners did not understand Him because they would not believe. The difficulty lay not so much in their inability as in their unwillingness. He knew moreover from the beginning of His earthly ministry that some of His professed followers would not believe on Him and that one of His disciples would betray Him. Of course, Jesus knew all this from eternity, but here it probably means that He was aware of it from the very beginning of His ministry on earth.

Now He explained that it was because of their unbelief that He had previously told them that no one could come to Him except it were given to him of the Father. Such words are an attack on human pride for man thinks he can earn or merit salvation. The Lord Jesus told men that even the power to come to Him can only be received from God the Father.

## Mixed Reactions to the Savior's Words (6:66-71)

These sayings of the Lord Jesus proved so distasteful to many who had followed Him that they now left Him and were no longer willing to associate with Him. As mentioned previously, these disciples were never true believers. They followed the Lord for various reasons, but not out of genuine love for Him and appreciation of who He was. At this point the Lord Jesus turned to the twelve disciples and challenged them with the question as to whether they, too, would leave Him (6:68). Peter said in effect, "Lord, how could we leave You? You teach the doctrines which lead to eternal life. If we leave You, there is no one else to whom we could go. To leave You would be to seal our doom." Speaking for the twelve, Peter further said that they had believed and had come to know that the Lord Jesus was the Holy One of God. Notice again the order of the words "believe and know." They had put their faith in the Lord Jesus Christ, and then they came to know that He was indeed all that He professed to be.

Peter had used the word "we" as meaning all twelve of the disciples, but the Lord Jesus corrected him. He should not say so confidently that all twelve were true believers. It is true that the Lord had chosen twelve disciples, but one of them was a devil. There was one in the company who did not share Peter's views concerning the Lord Jesus Christ. He knew that Judas would betray Him. He knew that Judas had never really accepted Him as Lord and Savior. Here again we have the all-knowledge of the Lord. Also, we have an evidence of the fact that Peter was not infallible when speaking for the twelve disciples.

CHAPTER

# 6

# MOUNTING CONTROVERSY (JOHN 7–8)

## Christ Rebukes His Brethren (7:1-9)

There was a lapse of some months between the events of chapters 6 and 7. The Lord remained in Galilee. He did not wish to stay in Judea because the Jews there sought to kill Him. The Jews referred to in verse 1 were the leaders or rulers. They were the ones who hated the Lord Jesus most bitterly, and who sought opportunities to slay Him.

The feast of the tabernacles mentioned in verse 2 was one of the important events in the Jewish calendar. It came at harvest time and celebrated the fact that the Jews lived in temporary shelters or booths after they came out of Egypt. It was a joyous festive occasion and looked forward to a coming day when the saved Jewish nation would dwell in the land of Israel, and when the Messiah would reign in peace and prosperity.

The Lord's brethren mentioned in verse 3 may have been sons born to Mary after the birth of Jesus or cousins or other distant relatives. But no matter how close their relationship to the Lord Jesus was, they were not thereby saved. They did not truly believe on Him. They told Him He should go to the feast of tabernacles in Jerusalem and perform some of His miracles there so that His disciples might see what He was doing. The disciples spoken of here were not the twelve, but those who professed to be followers of the Lord Jesus in Judea. Although they did not believe on Him, they wanted Him to manifest Himself openly perhaps so that attention would come to them as relatives of a famous person. Or more probably, they were jealous of His fame and wanted Him to go to Judea in hopes that He might be killed.

Perhaps the words of verse 4 were spoken in sarcasm. His relatives imply the Lord was looking for publicity. Why else was He performing all these miracles in Galilee if He did not want to become famous? "Now is your big opportunity," they say in effect. "You have been seeking to become famous. You should go to Jerusalem for the feast. Hundreds of people will be there, and You can do miracles for them. Galilee is a quiet place, and You are practically performing Your miracles in secret here. Why do You do this when we know that You want to become well known?" Then they added, "If you do these things, show yourself to the world." That is, "If You are really the Messiah, and if You are doing these miracles to prove it, why don't You offer these proofs where they will really count, namely, in Judea?" They had no sincere desire to see Him glorified. They did not really believe Him to be the Messiah. Neither were they willing to trust themselves to Him. What they said was said in sarcasm. Their hearts were not right before the Lord. It must have been especially bitter for the Lord Jesus to have His own brethren doubt His words and His works. Yet how often it is that those who are faithful to God find their bitterest opposition from those who are nearest and dearest to them.

The Lord's life was ordered from beginning to end (7:6). Each day and every movement was in accordance with a pre-arranged schedule. The time for manifesting Himself openly to the world had not yet come. He knew exactly what lay before Him, and it was not the will of God that He should go to Jerusalem at this time in order to make a public presentation of Himself. But He reminded His brethren that their time was always ready. Their lives were lived according to their own desires and not in obedience to the will of God. They could make their own plans and travel as they pleased, because they were only intent on doing their own will. The world could not hate the brothers of the Lord because they belonged to the world. They took their sides with the world against Jesus. Their whole lives were in harmony with the world. The world here refers to the system which man has built up and in which there is no room for God or for His Christ: the world of culture, art, education and religion. Judea was particularly the religious world, and it was the rulers of the Jews who hated Christ the most.

The world hated Christ because He testified concerning it, that its works were evil. It is a sad commentary on man's depraved nature that when a sinless Man came into the world, the world sought to slay Him. The perfection of Christ's life showed the imperfection of everyone else's. Man resented this exposure of himself and instead of repenting and crying to God for mercy, he sought to destroy the One who revealed his sin.

Not to be hated by the world; to be loved and flattered and caressed by the world—is one of the most terrible positions in which a Christian can find himself. 'What bad thing have I done,' asked the ancient sage, 'that he should speak well of me?' The absence of the world's hate proves that we do not testify against it that its works are evil. The warmth of the world's love proves that we are of its own. The friendship of the world is enmity with God. Whosoever therefore will be a friend of the world is the enemy of God (John 7:7; 15:19; James 4:4).

Verse 8 tells us that the Lord told His brethren to go up to the feast. There was something very sad about this. They pretended to be religious men. They were going to keep the feast of tabernacles. Yet the Christ of God was standing in their midst, and they had no real love for Him. Man loves religious rituals because he can observe them without any real heart interest. But bring him face to face with the Person of Christ and he is ill at ease. The Lord Jesus said that He would not go up to the feast as yet because His time had not yet full come. He did not mean He would not go to the feast at all, but that He would not go with His brethren and have a great and public manifestation. It was not time for that. When He would go, He would go quietly and with a minimum of publicity. So the Lord Jesus remained in Galilee after His brethren had gone up to the feast. They left behind the only One who could impart to them the joy and rejoicing of which the feast of tabernacles spoke.

## Jesus Teaches in the Temple (7:10-31)

Sometimes after His brethren had gone to Jerusalem, the Lord Jesus made a quiet trip there. As a devout Jew, He desired to attend the feast. But as the obedient Son of God, He could not do so openly but in secret. The Jews who sought Him at the feast were doubtless the rulers who sought to kill Him. When they asked, "Where is he?" they were not interested in worshipping Him, but in destroying Him. Verse 12 makes it clear that the Lord was creating quite a stir among the people. More and more, the miracles that He performed were compelling men to make up their minds as to who He really was. There was an undercurrent of conversation at the feast as to whether He was genuine or a false prophet. Some said He was a good Man. Others said that He deceived the people. But the opposition of the rulers against Jesus had become so intense that no one dared to speak openly in favor of Him. Doubtless many of the common people recognized that He was truly the Messiah of Israel, but they did not say it because they feared the leaders would persecute them.

The feast of tabernacles lasted for several days and in verse 14 we see a change because when the feast was about half over, the Lord Jesus went up to the outside area of the temple known as the porch where the people were allowed to gather and taught. Those who heard Him were amazed. Doubtless it was His knowledge of the Scriptures that impressed them most. But also the breadth of His learning and His ability to teach attracted their attention. They knew Jesus had never been to any of the great schools and they could not understand how He could have such an education as He did. The Lord refused to take any credit for Himself, but simply sought to glorify His Father. He answered that His teaching was not His own, but came from the One who sent Him. Whatever the Lord Jesus spoke and whatever He taught were the things that His Father told Him to speak and to teach. He did not act independently of the Father.

If the Jews really wanted to know whether His message was true or not, it would be easy to find out. If a man really wished to do God's will, then God would reveal to Him whether the teachings of Christ were divine or whether the Lord was simply teaching what He Himself wanted to teach. There is a wonderful promise here for everyone earnestly seeking the truth. If a man is sincere, if he truly wants to know what is the truth, God will reveal it to him. Anyone who speaks from himself, that is, according to his own will, seeks his own glory. But it was not so with the Lord Jesus. He sought the glory of the Father who had sent Him. Because His motives were absolutely pure, His message was absolutely true. There was no unrighteousness in Him. The Lord was the only One of whom such words could be spoken. Every other teacher has had some selfishness mixed in his service. However, it should be the ambition of every servant of the Lord to glorify God rather than self (7:18). In verse 19 the Lord then made a direct accusation against the Jews. He reminded them that Moses gave them the law. They gloried in the fact that they possessed the law but they forgot there was no virtue in merely possessing the law. The law demanded obedience to its commands. Although they gloried in the law, evidently none of them kept it for even then they were plotting to kill the Lord Jesus. The law expressly forbade killing or murder. They were breaking the law in their intentions concerning the Lord Jesus Christ. The Jews felt the sharp edge of Jesus' accusation but rather than admit He was true, they began to abuse Him. They said He was possessed of a demon. They challenged His statement that any of them sought to kill Him.

In verses 21 through 24 the Lord Jesus answers their question. He went back to the healing of the impotent man at the pool of Bethesda. It was this miracle that had stirred the hatred of the Jewish leaders against Him, and it was at this point that they began their vicious plot to kill Him. The Lord reminded them that He did one miracle, and they all "marveled" at it. The thought is not that they marveled at it with admiration, but that they were shocked He should do such a thing on the Sabbath day. The Law of Moses commanded that a male child should be circumcised eight days after birth. If the eighth day fell on the Sabbath, the Jews did not consider it wrong to circumcise the baby boy. They felt that it was a work of necessity and that the law allowed for such a work. If they circumcised a child on the Sabbath day, in order to obey the Law of Moses, why should they find fault with the Lord Jesus for making a man perfectly well on the Sabbath day? If the law allowed for a work of necessity, would it not also allow for a work of mercy?

The trouble with the Jews was that they judged things according to outward appearances and not according to inward reality. Their judgment was not righteous. Works that seemed perfectly legitimate when performed by them seemed wrong when performed by the Lord. Human nature always tends to judge according to sight rather than according to reality. The Lord had not broken the Law of Moses; it was they who were breaking it by their senseless hatred of Him.

We learn from verse 25 that by this time, it had become well known in Jerusalem that the Jewish leaders were plotting against the Savior. Here some of the common people asked if this was not the One whom their rulers were pursuing. They could not understand the Lord Jesus being allowed to speak so openly and fearlessly. If the rulers hated Him as much as the people had been led to believe, why did they allow Him to continue? Is it possible that they had come to find out that He was really the Messiah after all, as He claimed to be?

The people who did not believe Jesus to be the Messiah thought they knew where He came from. They believed He came from Nazareth. They knew His mother, Mary, and supposed that Joseph was His father. It was commonly believed by the Jews that when the Messiah came, He would come suddenly and mysteriously. They had no idea that He would be born as a Babe and grow up to be a Man. They should have known from the Old Testament that He would be born in Bethlehem, but they seemed quite ignorant of the details concerning the coming of the Messiah. That is why they said here in verse 27, "When the Christ comes, no one knows where He is from."

At this point Jesus cried out to the people who had gathered and who were listening to the conversation (7:28). They did indeed know Him, He said, and they knew where He came from. He was saying, of course, that they knew Him simply as a Man. They knew Him as Jesus of Nazareth. But what they did not know was that He was also God. They should realize that He did not come of Himself but had been sent from God the Father of whom these people were ignorant. Thus the Lord made a direct claim to equality with God. He had been sent into the world by the true God, and this God they did not know. But He knew Him. He dwelt with God from all eternity and was equal in all respects with God the Father. For when the Lord said He was from God, He did not simply mean that He was sent from God, but that He always lived with God and was equal with Him in all respects. In the expression "he has sent me," the Lord stated in the clearest possible way that He was the Christ of God, the anointed One, whom God had sent into the world to accomplish the work of redemption.

From verse 30 we know that the Jews understood the significance of Jesus' words and knew He was claiming to be the Messiah. They considered this to be blasphemy and attempted to arrest Him but were not able to lay their hands on Him because His hour was not yet come.

Actually many of the people did believe on the Lord Jesus. We would like to think that their belief was genuine. Their reasoning was this. What more could Jesus do to prove He was the Messiah? When the Messiah came, if Jesus was not the Messiah, would He be able to do more numerous or more wonderful miracles than Jesus had done? Obviously they believed the miracles of Jesus proved Him to be the real Messiah.

## Enmity of the Pharisees (7:32-36)

As the Pharisees moved in and out among the people, they heard this undercurrent of conversation. The people were murmuring about the Savior, not in the sense of complaining against Him, but secretly revealing their admiration for Him. The Pharisees were afraid that this might become a great movement to accept Jesus, and so they sent officers to arrest Him. The words of verses 33 and 34 were undoubtedly spoken to these officers as well as to the Pharisees and to the people in general.

The Lord reminded them He would only be with them for a little while, and then He would go back to God the Father who sent Him. Undoubtedly this only made the Pharisees the more angry. In a coming day, the Lord said, the Pharisees would seek Him and would not be able to find Him. There would come a time when they would need the Savior, but it would be too late. He would have gone back to heaven, and because of their unbelief and wickedness, they would not be able to meet Him there. The words of this verse are especially solemn. There is such a thing as the passing of opportunity. Men might have the opportunity to be saved today; if they reject it, they might never have the opportunity again.

The Jews failed to understand the meaning of the Lord's words. They did not realize He was going back to heaven. They thought that perhaps He was going on a preaching tour, ministering to the Jewish people who were scattered among the Gentiles, and also perhaps even teaching the Gentiles themselves. They expressed their wonder at His words. What did He mean when He said that they would seek Him and would not be able to find Him? Where could He go without their being able to follow Him?

## The Promise of the Holy Spirit (7:37-39)

In this section we come to the last day of the feast. The Jewish people had gone through this religious observance, and yet their hearts were not satisfied because they had not truly understood the deep meaning of the feast. Just before they departed for their homes, the Lord Jesus stood and cried out to them. He invited them to come to Him for spiritual satisfaction. Pay particular attention to the words. His invitation was extended to "any man." His was a universal gospel. Anyone could be saved if he would simply come to Christ. But notice the condition. The Scripture says, "If any man thirst." "Thirst" here, of course, speaks of spiritual need. Unless a man knows he is a sinner, he will not want to be saved. Unless he realizes he is lost, he will not desire to be found. Unless a man is conscious of a great spiritual lack in his life, he will not want to go to the Lord to have that need supplied. The Savior invited the thirsting soul to come to Him—not the church, the preacher, the waters of baptism, or to the Lord's Table. "Come unto me," He said. "Come unto me, and *drink.*" To "drink" means to appropriate Christ for oneself—to trust Him as Savior and Lord.

Verse 38 proves that to come to Christ and "drink" is the same as to *believe* on Him. All who believe on Him will have their own needs supplied and will receive rivers of blessing enough to flow out to others. All through the Old Testament it was taught that those who accepted the Messiah would be helped themselves and would be channels of blessing to others. The expression "out of his belly shall flow rivers of living water" means out of a person's inner life would flow streams of help to others. It is clearly stated that "living water" refers to the Holy Spirit. Verse 39 is important because it teaches that all who receive the Lord Jesus Christ also receive the Spirit of God. At the time the Lord Jesus spoke, the Holy Spirit had not been given. It was not until after the Lord Jesus went back to heaven and was glorified there that the Holy Spirit descended on the day of Pentecost. From that moment on, every true believer in the Lord Jesus Christ has been permanently indwelt by the Holy Ghost.

## Divided Opinion Concerning Christ (7:40-53)

Some of those who listened were now convinced that the Lord Jesus was the Prophet of whom Moses spoke in Deuteronomy 18:15, 18. Some were even willing to acknowledge that Jesus was the Christ, or the Messiah. But others thought this was impossible. They believed that Jesus came from Nazareth in Galilee, and there was no prophecy in the Old Testament indicating the Messiah would come out of Galilee. The Jews were right in believing the Messiah would come from Bethlehem and that He would be descended from David. Had they taken the trouble to inquire, they would have found that Jesus was born in Bethlehem, and that He was a direct descendant of David. Because of these differing opinions and because of the general ignorance there was a division among the people because of Christ. It is still the same. Men and women are divided on the subject of Jesus. Some say He was simply a Man like the rest of us. Others are willing to admit that He was the greatest Man who ever lived. But those who believe the Word of God know that the Lord Jesus Christ is God over all, blessed forever.

Efforts were still being made to arrest the Lord but no one was successful in taking Him (7:44). As long as a person is walking in the will of God, no power on earth can hinder him. "We are immortal until our work is done."

The Lord Jesus' time had not yet come, and so men were unable to harm Him. We read in verse 32 that the Pharisees and the chief priests had sent officers to arrest Jesus. In verse 45 the officers had returned, but did not have the Lord with them. The chief priests and Pharisees were annoyed and asked the officers why they had not brought Him. The officers were compelled to speak well of the Savior, even though they did not accept Him themselves. "No man ever spoke like this man," they said. Doubtless they had listened to many men in their day, but they had never heard anyone speak with such authority, wisdom, and grace. In an effort to intimidate the officers, the Pharisees accused them of being deceived by Jesus. They reminded them that none of the rulers of the Jewish nation had trusted on Christ. What a terrible argument this was! It was to their shame that leading men in the Jewish nation had failed to recognize the Messiah. These Pharisees were not only unwilling to believe on the Lord Jesus themselves, but they did not want others to believe on Him either. So it is today. Many who do not want to be saved themselves do everything in their power to prevent their relatives and friends from being saved, too.

After attacking the Officers, the Pharisees in verse 49 spoke of the mass of the Jewish people as ignorant and cursed. Their argument was that if the common people knew anything at all about the Scriptures, they would know that Jesus was not the Messiah. They could not have been more wrong. At this point Nicodemus spoke. Apparently Nicodemus had previously come to Jesus, had trusted the Lord and had been saved. Here he stepped forward, among the rulers of the Jews, to say a word for his Lord. He claimed the Jews had not given Jesus a fair chance. Jewish law did not condemn a man before it heard his case, yet this was what the Jewish leaders were doing. Were they afraid of the facts? Now the rulers turned on Nicodemus who was one of their own company and asked with a sneer if he was also one of the Galilaean followers of Jesus. Did he not know that the Old Testament never spoke of a prophet as coming out of Galilee? In this they showed their own ignorance. Had they never read of the prophet Jonah? He had come from Galilee.

The feast of tabernacles was now over. The men returned to their own homes. Some had met the Savior face to face and had trusted in Him. But the vast majority had rejected Him, and the leaders of the Jewish people were more determined than ever to do away with Him. They considered Him a threat to their religion and to their way of life.

## The Woman Taken in Adultery (8:1-11)

The first verse of chapter 8 is closely linked with the last verse of the previous chapter. The connection is better seen by putting the two verses together as follows—"And everyone went to his own house. But Jesus went to the Mount of Olives." The Lord had truly said, "Foxes have holes, and the birds of the air have nests, but the Son of man has nowhere to lay his head." The Mount of Olives of course was not far from the temple. In the morning the Lord walked back down the side of Olivet, crossed the vale of Kidron and so on back to the city, where the temple was located. A great multitude of people came to Him, and He sat down and began to instruct them again.

Before we review these verses it should be mentioned that the passage of chapter 7:53, through chapter 8:11, does not appear in all the ancient manuscripts of the Bible. There is some question as to whether these verses form a part of the original text. The author believes that it is proper to accept them as part of the inspired text because all that they teach is in perfect agreement with the rest of the Bible.

In verse 3 we read that the scribes (a group of men who copied and taught the Scriptures) and the Pharisees tried to trap the Lord Jesus so they would have some charge to bring against Him. They had caught a woman in the very act of adultery, and they brought her and made her stand in the middle of the crowd, probably facing Jesus. The accusation against the woman was doubtless true. She was caught while committing this sin. (The word "Master" in this verse means "Teacher.") Verse 5 records the words that the accusers used to try to trap the Lord. They wanted the Lord to contradict the sayings of Moses. If they could succeed in doing that, then they could turn the common people against Him. They reminded the Lord that Moses commanded that a person taken in the act of adultery should be stoned to death. For their own wicked purposes, the Pharisees hoped the Lord would disagree, and so they asked Him what He had to say on the subject. Justice and the Law of Moses, thought they, demand that she should be stoned to death. As someone has said, "It comforts and quiets the depraved heart of man if he can only find a person worse than himself: he thinks the greater sin of another excuses himself; and while accusing and vehemently blaming another, he forgets his own evil. He thus rejoices in iniquity."

They had no real charge against the Lord and were trying to manufacture one (8:6). If He let the woman go free, He would be opposing the Law of Moses and they would accuse Him of being unjust. If He condemned the woman to death, then they could say that He was not merciful. The Lord Jesus stooped down and wrote with His finger on the ground. There is no way of knowing what He wrote. Dissatisfied, the Jews insisted He make some reply. Verse seven records the masterful reply of Jesus. The Lord suggested the penalty of the law be carried out, but that it be done by those who had committed no sin. Thus the Lord upheld the Law of Moses and at the same time accused every one of having sinned themselves. Those who wish to judge others should be pure themselves. This verse is sometimes used to excuse sin. The attitude is that we are free from blame because everyone has done things that are wrong. But this verse does not excuse sin. It condemns those who are guilty even though they have never been caught.

Once again the Savior stooped down and wrote on the ground. Verses 6 and 8 are the only recorded instances of the Lord Jesus writing anything and what He wrote has long been erased from the earth. Those who accused the woman were convicted (8:9). They had nothing to say. One by one they began to go away. All were guilty, from the oldest to the youngest. Jesus was left standing alone, with the woman nearby. Then in wonderful grace, the Lord Jesus pointed out to the woman that all her accusers had vanished. They were nowhere to be found. Not a single person had dared to condemn her. "Has no one condemned you?" He asked. She said, "No one, Lord." The word "Lord" here means "Sir." When the woman said, "No one, Sir," the Lord uttered those wonderful words, "Neither do I condemn you: go and sin no more." The Lord did not claim to have civil authority in this matter. This power was vested in the Roman government, and He left it there. But He did issue a warning to her that she should refrain from sinning.

In the first chapter of this Gospel, we learned that "grace and truth came by Jesus Christ." Here was an example of that. In the words "neither do I condemn thee," we have an example of grace; the words "go and sin no more" are words of truth. The Lord did not say, "Go, and sin as little as possible." Jesus Christ is God, and His standard is absolute perfection. He cannot approve of sin in any degree. And so He set before her the perfect standard of God Himself.

## "I am the Light of the World" (8:12-20)

The scene now changed to the treasury of the temple, as we shall learn in verse 20. A multitude was still following the Lord. He turned to them and made one of the many grand statements as to His Messiahship. He said, "I am the light of the world." The world is in the darkness of sin, ignorance and aimlessness. The Light of the world is Jesus. Apart from Him, there is no deliverance from the blackness of sin, no guidance along the way of life and no knowledge of the real meaning of life, and the issues of eternity. Jesus promised that anyone following Him would not walk in darkness, but would have the light of life. To follow Jesus means to believe on Him. Many people think they can live as Jesus lived without being born again. But to follow Jesus means to come to Him in repentance, to trust Him as Lord and Savior, and then to commit one's whole life to Him. Those who do this have guidance in life and a clear, bright hope beyond the grave.

The Pharisees, in verse 13, challenged Jesus on a legal point. They reminded Him He was testifying concerning Himself. A person's own testimony was not considered sufficient because the average human being is biased. The Pharisees did not mind casting doubt on the words of Jesus. In fact they doubted if His words were true at all. Verses 14 to 18 record Jesus' response. The Lord recognized that usually it was necessary to have two or three witnesses. But in His case, His testimony was absolutely true because He is God. He knew He had come from heaven and was going back to heaven. But they did not know where He had come from nor where He was going. They thought He was just another man like themselves and would not believe that He was the eternal Son, equal with the Father. They judged by outward appearances and according to merely human standards. They looked upon Jesus as the Carpenter of Nazareth and never stopped to think He was different from any other man who ever lived.

The Lord Jesus said that He judged no man (8:15). This may mean that He did not judge men according to worldly standards, like the Pharisees did. Or more probably it meant that His purpose in coming into the world was not to judge men but to save them. If the Lord were to judge, His judgment would be righteous and true. He is God and everything He does is done in partnership with the Father who sent Him. Over and over again, the Lord Jesus emphasized to the Pharisees His unity with God the Father. It was this that stirred up in their hearts the bitterest antagonism to Him. The Lord acknowledged that the testimony of two witnesses was required by the Law of Moses. Nothing He had said was intended to deny that. So, if they insisted on having two witnesses, it was not difficult to produce them. First of all, He bore witness of Himself by His sinless life and by the words that came out of His mouth. Secondly, the Father bore witness to Him by public statements from heaven and by the miracles that He gave the Lord to do. The Lord Jesus fulfilled the prophecies of the Old Testament concerning the Messiah, and yet in face of this strong evidence, the Jewish leaders were unwilling to believe.

The Pharisees' next question, contained in verse 19, was doubtless spoken in scorn. Perhaps they looked around the crowd as they said, "Where is thy Father?" The Lord Jesus answered that they did not recognize who He truly was. Neither did they know His Father. Of course, they would have denied such ignorance of God, but it was true. If they had received the Lord Jesus, they would have known the Father, too. But no man can know God the Father except through the Lord Jesus. Thus, their rejection of Him made it impossible for them to honestly claim that they knew and loved God. The scene of this encounter was the treasury of the temple. Again the Lord was divinely protected and no man could lay hands on Him to arrest Him or to kill Him. His hour had not yet come. The "hour," of course, refers to the time when He would be crucified at Calvary to die for the sins of the world.

## Jesus Predicts His Departure (8:21-30)

Once again in verse 21 the Lord showed perfect knowledge of the future. He told His critics He was going to go away—referring not only to His death and burial, but to His resurrection and ascension back to heaven. The Jewish people would continue to seek for the Messiah, not realizing that He had already come and been rejected. Because of their rejection, they would die in their sins and would be forever prevented from entering heaven, where the Lord was going. It is a solemn truth! Those who refuse to accept the Lord Jesus have no hope of heaven. How solemn it is to die in one's sins, without God, without Christ, without hope forever.

The Jews did not understand that the Lord spoke of going back to heaven (8:22). What did He mean by "going away"? Did He mean He would escape from their plot to kill Him by committing suicide? It was strange they should think this. If He were to kill Himself, there would be nothing to prevent them from doing the same and following Him. It was just another example of the darkness of unbelief. It seems amazing they could be so dull and ignorant of what the Savior was saying! Doubtless referring to their foolish reference to suicide, the Lord told them that they were from beneath, that is, they had a very low outlook on things and could not rise above the literal things of time and sense. They had no spiritual understanding. The Lord Jesus, in contrast, was from above. His thoughts, words, and deeds were heavenly. All that they did savored of the world; His whole life proclaimed Him to be from a purer land than this world.

The Lord often used repetition for emphasis. So in verse 24 He warned again that they would die in their sins. If they steadfastly refused to believe on Him, there was no alternative. Apart from the Lord Jesus, there is no way to obtain forgiveness of sins and those who die with sins unforgiven cannot enter heaven. The word "he" does not belong in this verse. It reads "If you believe not that I am, you shall die in your sins." We see in the words "I am," another claim to deity by the Lord Jesus.

The Jews were completely perplexed. They asked Him pointedly who He was. Perhaps they meant this in sarcasm, as if to say, "Who do You think You are?" Or perhaps they were really anxious to hear what He would say concerning Himself. His answer is worthy of note. He said, "Even the same that I said unto you from the beginning." From the outset of His earthly ministry, the Lord had told men He was the promised Messiah. The Jews had heard Him say so frequently, but their stubborn hearts refused to bow to the truth. But His answer can be taken another way—the Lord Jesus was exactly what He preached. He did not say one thing and do another. He was the living embodiment of all that He taught. His life agreed with His teaching.

The meaning of verse 26 is not clear. It seems the Lord was saying there were many additional things He could say and judge concerning these unbelieving Jews. He could expose the wicked thoughts and motives of their hearts. However, He was obediently speaking only those things which the Father had given Him to speak. And since the Father is true, He is worthy to be believed and to be listened to. The Jews did not understand Him. Their minds were becoming more clouded all the time. Previously when the Lord Jesus claimed to be the Son of God, they realized He was claiming equality with God the Father. But not so any more.

In verse 28 we again see Jesus prophesying about the future. He told them they would lift up the Son of man. This referred to His death by crucifixion on the cross. After they had done that, they would know indeed

He was the Messiah. They would know it by the earthquake and by the darkness, but, most of all, by His resurrection from the dead. Notice carefully the words of the Lord, "Then you will know that I am He." Here, again, the word "he" is not in the original. The Lord Jesus was saying, "Then you will know that I am." The meaning really is, "Then you will know that I am God." Then they would understand He did nothing from Himself, that is, by His own authority. He came into the world as the dependent One, speaking only those things that the Father had taught Him to speak.

The Lord's relationship with God the Father was very intimate. Each of the expressions in verse 29 was a claim to equality with God. Throughout all of His earthly ministry, the Father was with Him. At no time was Jesus left alone. At all times He did the things that were pleasing to God. These words could only be spoken by a sinless being. No man born of human parents could truthfully utter such words as these—"I always do those things that please Him." We do things that please ourselves or that please our fellow men. Only the Lord Jesus was completely taken up with the things that were well-pleasing to God. After saying this the Lord found many professed to believe on Him and doubtless some were genuine in their faith (8:30). Others might only have been giving lip service to the Lord.

## The Truth Shall Make You Free (8:31-36)

Jesus made a distinction in verses 31 and 32 between those who are disciples and those who are "disciples indeed." A disciple is anyone who professes to be a learner, but a "disciple indeed" is one who has definitely committed himself to Christ. True believers have this characteristic—they continue in His Word, that is they continue in His teachings. They do not turn aside from Him. True faith always has the quality of permanence. We are not saved by continuing in His Word, but we continue in His Word because we are saved.

The promise is now made to every true disciple that he will know the truth, and the truth will make him free. The Jews did not know the truth, and were in terrible bondage to ignorance, error, sin, law and superstition. Those who truly know the Lord Jesus are delivered from sin, they walk in the light, and are led by the Holy Spirit of God. Some of the Jews who were standing by heard the Lord's reference to being made free. They resented it immediately. They boasted of their descent from Abraham and said that they had never been in bondage (8:33). But that was not true. Israel had been in bondage to Egypt, Assyria, Babylon, Persia, Greece, and now Rome. But even more than that, the Jews were in bondage to sin and to Satan and this is what the Lord Jesus was speaking about. He reminded His listeners that those who practice sin are the slaves of sin (8:34). These Jews pretended to be very religious, but the truth of the matter was they were dishonest, irreverent, and intending murderers—for even now they were plotting the death of the Son of God.

Jesus next compared the relative positions in a house of a slave and a son. The slave did not have any assurance he would live there forever; the son was at home in the house. Does the word "Son" apply to the Son of God or to those who become children of God by faith in the Lord Jesus? Whichever view is accepted, the Lord Jesus was telling these Jews they were not sons, but slaves. There is no question that the word "Son" in verse 36 refers to Christ Himself. Those who are made free by Him are made free indeed. When a person comes to the Savior and receives eternal life from Him, that person is freed from the slavery of sin, legalism, superstition, and demonism.

## Abraham's Seed and Satan's (8:37-47)

The Lord now acknowledged that, as far as physical descent was concerned, these Jews were Abraham's seed. They could trace their lineage back to Abraham. But it was evident they were not of the spiritual seed of Abraham. They were not godly men like Abraham was. They sought to kill the Lord Jesus because they did not allow His words to take effect in their lives. They resisted His doctrines and would not yield to Him. The things Jesus taught them were things He had been commissioned by His Father to speak. He and His Father were so completely one that the words He spoke were the words of God the Father. The Lord Jesus perfectly represented His Father while here on the earth. In contrast, the Jews did those things which they had learned from *their* father. The Lord Jesus did not mean their literal, earthly father, but *the devil.*

In verse 39 the Jews once again claimed kinship to Abraham and boasted that Abraham was their father. The Lord Jesus pointed out that they did not have the characteristics of Abraham's children. Children look, walk, and talk like their parents but not so these Jews. Their lives were the opposite of Abraham's. Though children of Abraham according to the flesh, morally they were children of the devil. The difference between them and Abraham was evident. Jesus had come into the world, speaking the truth. They were offended and stumbled by His teaching, and tried to kill Him. Abraham never did this. He always took his place on the side of truth and righteousness. It was very clear who their father was because they acted just like him. Their father was the devil. The words of the Jews in verse 41 seem to be accusing the Lord of being born of fornication. Most Bible students, however, see in the word "fornication" a reference to idolatry. The Jews were saying they had never committed spiritual adultery. They had always been true to God. He is the only One whom they ever acknowledged as their Father.

The Lord showed the falseness of their claim, in verse 42, by reminding them that if they loved God, they would love Him whom God had sent. It is foolish to claim to love God and at the same time to hate the Lord Jesus Christ. Jesus said He came forth from God—that is He was the eternally begotten Son of God. This relationship of Son to the Father existed from all eternity. He also reminded the Jews that He came forth from God. Obviously, He was stating His pre-existence. He dwelt in heaven with the Father long before He appeared on this earth. But the Father sent Him into the world to be the Savior of the world, and so He came as the obedient One.

There is a difference in verse 43 between "speech" and "word." Christ's *word* referred to the things He taught. His *speech* referred to the words with which He expressed His truths. They could not even understand His speech. When He spoke of bread, they thought of literal bread. When He spoke of water, they thought of literal water. Why could they not understand His speech? It was because they were unwilling to tolerate His teachings.

Now the Lord Jesus came out openly in verse 44 and told them the devil was their father. This did not mean they had been born of the devil in the way believers are born of God. It meant, as Augustine said, they were children of the devil by imitation. They showed their relationship to the devil by living the way he lived. "The desires of your father you want to do." It is an expression of the intention and desire of their hearts.

The devil was a murderer from the beginning. He brought death to Adam and the whole human race. Not only was he a murderer, he was a liar as well. He did not stand in the truth because there is no truth in him. When he told a lie, he was merely expressing his nature. Lies formed a part of his very existence. He is a liar, and is the father of lies. The Jews imitated the devil in these two ways. They were murderers because their intention was to kill the Son of God. They were liars because they said God was their

Father. They pretended to be godly, spiritual men, but their lives were lives of wickedness. Those who give themselves over to lying seem to lose the capacity for discerning the truth. The Lord Jesus had always spoken the truth to these men. Yet they would not believe Him. This showed that their real character was wicked.

Only Christ, the sinless Son of God, could truly utter words like these recorded in verse 46. Not a person in the world could convict Him of a single sin. There was no defect in His character. He was perfect in all His ways. He spoke only words of truth, and yet they would not believe Him. If a man really loves God, he will hear and obey the words of God. The Jews showed by their rejection of the Savior's message that they did not really belong to God.

## Before Abraham was, I am (8:48-59)

In verse 48 we see that once again the Jews resorted to abusive language, because they could not answer the Lord in any other way. In calling Him "a Samaritan," they used a word of reproach. It was as if they said that He was a half-breed, not a pure Jew. Also, they accused Him of having a devil (demon). By this they doubtless meant He was mad or insane. To them, only a man out of his mind would make the claims Jesus had been making. Notice in verse 49 the even-tempered way the Lord answered His enemies. His words were not those of one who had a devil, but of One who sought to honor God the Father. It was for this they were dishonoring Him, not because He was demon possessed, but because He was completely taken up with the interests of His Father in heaven.

They should have known that at no time did He seek His own glory. All He did was calculated to bring glory to His Father (8:50). Even though He accused them of dishonoring Him, that did not mean that He was seeking His own glory. Then the Lord Jesus added the words, "There is One who seeks and judges." This referred, of course, to God. God the Father would seek glory for His beloved Son, and would judge all of those who failed to give Him this glory.

In verse 51 we have one of those majestic sayings of the Lord Jesus, words that could only be uttered by One who was God Himself. The words are introduced by the familiar expression "Most Assuredly, I say to you." The Lord Jesus promised that if a man kept His saying, that man would never see death. This cannot refer to physical death because many believers in the Lord Jesus die each day. The reference is to spiritual death. The Lord was saying that those who believe on Him are delivered from eternal death and shall never suffer the pangs of hell.

The Jews were more convinced than ever that Jesus was mad. We read in verse 52 that they reminded Him that Abraham and the prophets were all dead. Yet He had said that if a man kept His sayings he would not see death. How could these things be reconciled? They realized the Lord was claiming to be greater than Abraham and the prophets. Abraham never delivered anyone from death, and could not deliver himself from death. Neither could the prophets. Yet here was One who claimed to be able to deliver His fellow men from death. He must consider Himself greater than the fathers.

The Jews thought Jesus was seeking to attract attention to Himself (8:54). He reminded them that this was not the case. It was God the Father who was honoring Him, the very God whom they professed to love and serve. The Jews said God was their Father, but actually they did not know Him. Yet here they were speaking with One who did know the Father, One who was equal with Him. They wanted Jesus to deny His equality with the Father, but He said if He did this, He would be a liar. He knew God the Father and obeyed His words.

Since the Jews insisted on bringing Abraham into the argument, the Lord reminded them in verse 56 that Abraham had looked forward to the day of the Messiah, and he had actually seen it by faith, and was glad. And He was the One to whom Abraham looked forward. Abraham's faith rested in the coming of Christ. Thus the Lord Jesus claimed to be the fulfillment of all the prophecies in the Old Testament concerning the Messiah.

The next verse (v. 57) reminds us again of the Jews inability to understand divine truth. "He had said, 'Abraham rejoiced *to see my day . . .'* but they replied as though He had said that *He had seen Abraham.*" There is a great difference here. The Lord was really claiming for Himself a position greater than Abraham. He was the Object of Abraham's thoughts and hopes. Abraham looked forward by faith to Christ's day. The Jews could not understand this. They reasoned that Jesus was not yet fifty years old. (Actually He was only about thirty-three years of age at this time.) How could He have seen Abraham?

In verse 58 the Lord made another clear claim to be God. He did not say, "Before Abraham was, I was." That might simply mean that He came into existence before Abraham. Rather, He used the Name of God, I AM. The Lord had dwelt with God the Father from all eternity. There was never a time when He came into being, or when He did not exist. Therefore He said, "Before Abraham was, I am." At once the wicked Jews attempted to put Jesus to death, but in a miraculous way He moved out of their midst and left the temple. The Jews understood exactly what Jesus meant when He said, "Before Abraham was, I am." He was claiming to be Jehovah. It was for this reason they sought to stone Him, because to them this was blasphemy. They were unwilling to accept the fact that the Messiah was in their midst. They would not have Him to reign over them.

CHAPTER

# 7

# THE GOOD SHEPHERD (JOHN 9–10)

## The Sixth Sign: Healing of the Man Born Blind (9:1-12)

This incident recorded in chapter 9 may have taken place as Jesus was leaving the temple area, or it may have occurred some time after the events of chapter 8. We are told in verse one that the man had been born blind to emphasize the hopelessness of his condition and the wonder of the miracle that gave him sight.

The disciples asked a rather strange question in verse two. They wondered if the blindness had been caused by the man's own sin or by the sin of his parents. How could the blindness have been caused by his own sin, when he had been *born* blind? Did they believe in some form of reincarnation? Or might the man have been born blind because of sins which God knew he would commit after his birth? It is clear they thought the blindness was directly connected with sin in the family. But this was not necessarily so. Although all sickness, suffering, and death came into the world as a result of sin, it is not true that in any particular case a person suffers because of sins which he has committed. Jesus told the disciples that the blindness was not a direct result of sin in the lives of either the man or his parents. God had allowed this man to be born blind so that the mighty works of God might be displayed. Before the man was born, the Lord Jesus knew He would give sight to those blind eyes. He knew too that He had only about three years of public ministry before He would be crucified. Every moment of that time must be spent in working for God. Here was a man who had been blind from his birth. The Lord Jesus must perform a miracle of healing on him, even though it was the Sabbath day. The time of His public ministry would soon be over, and He would no longer be here on earth, performing such mighty works. This is a solemn reminder to us too that life's day is swiftly passing, and the night is coming when our service on earth will be over forever. We should use the time given to us to serve the Lord acceptably.

When Jesus was in the world as a Man, He was the Light of the world in a very direct and special way (9:5). He performed miracles and taught the people. The Light of the world was before their very eyes. Jesus is still the Light of the world, and all who come to Him are promised they will not walk in darkness. However, in this verse the Lord was speaking particularly of His public ministry on earth.

We are not told why Jesus mixed clay and spittle and put it on the blind man's eyes (9:6). Some have suggested the man had no eyeballs and that the Lord simply created them. Others suggest the Lord deliberately used methods despised in the eyes of the world. He used weak and insignificant things in working out His purposes. Even today, in giving sight to the spiritually blind, God uses men and women, who are made of the dust of the earth.

In verse 7 the Lord called into operation the faith of the blind man by telling him to go and wash in the pool of Siloam. No doubt he knew the location of the pool and was able to do as he was told. The Scripture notes that the word "Siloam" means "Sent." Perhaps this is a reference to the Messiah, the "Sent One." The One who was performing this miracle was the One who had been sent into the world by the Father. The blind man went and washed in the pool and received his sight. He had never seen before at all! The miracle was instantaneous and the man was able to use his eyes immediately. What a delightful surprise it must have been for him to look for the first time upon the world in which he had lived!

The friends of the man were startled. They could hardly believe this was the same man who had begged for so long. (It should be this way also when a person is saved. Our neighbors should be able to notice the difference in us.) Some insisted it was the same man. Others, not quite so sure, were only willing to admit there was a resemblance. But the man removed all doubt by stating that he was the one who had been born blind.

Whenever Jesus performed a miracle, it provoked all kinds of questions. Often these questions gave the believer an opportunity to witness for the Lord. Here people asked the man how it all happened. His testimony was simple, yet convincing. He recited the facts of his healing, giving credit to the One who had performed the miracle. At this time, the man did not realize who the Lord Jesus was. He simply referred to Him as "a man that is called Jesus." But later on the man's understanding grows and he comes to know who Jesus is. The man's questioners then wanted to know where Jesus could be found. When we witness concerning the Lord Jesus Christ, we create a desire in the hearts of others to come to know Him, too.

## The Increasing Opposition of the Jews (9:13-34)

Some of the Jewish people probably in earnest enthusiasm over the miracle brought the blind man to the Pharisees. They probably did not realize how the leaders of the Jewish people would resent what had happened. Jesus had performed the miracle on the Sabbath day. The critical Pharisees did not realize that God never intended the Sabbath to prevent an act of mercy or of kindness.

In verse 15 the man had another opportunity to witness for Jesus. The Pharisees asked him how he had received his sight, and they heard the simple story once again. The man did not mention the name of Jesus here, probably not because he was afraid to do so, but because he realized now that everyone knew who had done this mighty work. By this time, the Lord Jesus was well known in Jerusalem.

Another division arose over who Jesus was (9:16). Some of the Pharisees announced that Jesus could not be a godly Man because He had broken the Sabbath. Others reasoned that a sinful man could not perform such a wonderful miracle. Jesus often caused divisions among people. Men were forced to take sides and be either for Him or against Him. The Pharisees, in verse 17, asked the man who had been blind what he thought of Jesus. As yet, he did not realize that Jesus was God. But his faith had grown to the point of admitting that Jesus was a Prophet. He believed that the One who had given him sight had been sent by God, and had a divine message.

Despite the testimony of the man, we read in verse 18 that many of the Jews, presumably the Pharisees, were still unwilling to believe a miracle had been performed. So they called the parents of the man to see what they would say. Who would know better than parents if a child had been born without sight? Surely their testimony would be conclusive. The Pharisees therefore asked them whether this was their son and also how he received his sight. The testimony of the parents was positive. This was their son and they knew through years of heartache he had always been blind. Beyond that, they were unwilling to go. They did not know how he received his sight, they said, or who the person was who gave it. They directed the Pharisees back to the son himself (9:23). He could speak for himself. They had heard that any man confessing Jesus to be Messiah would be put out of the synagogue. This excommunication was a very serious matter for any Jew. They were not willing to pay such a price. It would mean the loss of a means of livelihood, as well as a loss of all the privileges of the Jewish religion. It was for fear of the Jewish rulers, therefore, that the parents shifted the testimony back to their son.

The expression in verse 24 "Give God the glory" may have two meanings. First of all, it may be a form of oath. Perhaps the Pharisees were saying, "Now tell the truth. We know that this man is a sinner." Or possibly the Pharisees were demanding that God be given the glory for the miracle, and no credit be given to Jesus because they considered Him a sinful man. The Pharisees met failure at every turn. Every time they tried to discredit the Lord Jesus, it resulted in bringing more honor to Him. The man's testimony was beautiful. He did not know much about Jesus, but he did know that, once he was blind, now he could see! This was a testimony no one could deny. So it is in the case of those who have been born again. The world may doubt, and scoff, and sneer, but no one can deny our testimony when we say that once we were lost, and now we have been saved by the grace of God.

In verse 26 the Pharisees reopened the questioning, asking him to repeat the details. The man who had been blind was getting annoyed. He reminded them he had already told them the facts and they did not believe what he

said. Why did they want to hear it again? Did they want to become disciples of Jesus? Obviously, this was asked in sarcasm! He knew very well they hated Jesus, and had no desire to follow Him. It has been said, "When you have no case, abuse the plaintiff." That is what happened here. The Pharisees had failed to shake the testimony of this man, so they began to abuse him. They accused him of being a disciple of Jesus, as if that were the worst thing in the world. Then they professed to be Moses' disciples, as if that were the greatest thing possible. The Pharisees said that God had spoken to

Moses and then spoke slightingly of Jesus. Had they believed Moses, they would have accepted the Lord Jesus. Moreover, Moses never gave sight to a man who had been born blind. A greater than Moses was in their midst, and they did not know it.

In verse 30 the sarcasm of the one whose eyes had been opened now became biting. It was something the Pharisees didn't expect. The man said in effect, "You are the teachers of the Jewish people. And yet here is a Man in your midst who has the power to give sight to blind eyes, and you do not know where He comes from. Shame on you."

He was now becoming bolder in his witness. His faith was growing. He reminded them that as a general principle, God does not hear sinners or work miracles through them. God does not approve of men who are evil, and does not give power to such men to perform mighty works. But, on the other hand, worshippers of God receive God's commendation and are assured of God's approval. This man realized he was the first man in all of human history to be born blind and to receive sight. He could not understand how the Pharisees could witness such a miracle and find fault with the Person who performed it (9:32). If the Lord Jesus were not of God, He could never have done a miracle of this nature.

We read again in verse 34 that the Pharisees turned to abuse. They insinuated that this man's blindness was the direct result of sin. What right had he to teach them? The truth is he had every right for, as someone has said, "The teaching of the Holy Ghost is more frequently to be seen among men of low degree, than among men of rank and education." "They cast him out," we read in verse 34. This probably refers to more than his being cast out of the temple. It probably means that he was excommunicated from the Jewish religion. And yet what was the ground for the excommunication? A man born blind had been given his sight on the Sabbath day. Because he would not speak evil of the One who had performed the miracle, he was excommunicated.

## Spiritual Blindness (9:35-41)

Jesus now sought out this man. In effect He said to him, "If they do not want you, I will take you." Those who are cast out for Jesus' sake lose nothing, but gain a great blessing in His personal welcome and fellowship. See how the Lord Jesus led the man to personal faith in Himself as the Son of God! He simply asked the question, "Do you believe on the Son of God?"

Although he had received his physical sight, the man was still in need of spiritual sight. He asked the Lord who the Son of God was that he might believe on Him. In using the word "Lord" here, the man was simply saying "Sir." The Lord Jesus now introduced Himself as the Son of God. It was not a mere man who had given him sight. It was not a mere man who had performed the impossible in his life. It was the Son of God, the One whom he had seen and who was now speaking with him. At this the man simply and sweetly placed his faith in the Lord Jesus and fell down and worshipped Him (9:38). He was now a saved soul as well as a healed man. What a great day this had been in his life! He had received both physical and spiritual sight. Notice he did not worship the Lord until he knew Him to be the Son of God. Being an intelligent Jew, he would not worship a mere man. But as soon as he learned that the One who healed him was God, he worshipped Him—not for what He had done but for who He was.

At first glance verse 39 seems to contradict John 3:17, "For God did not send His Son into the world to condemn the world . . . ." But there is no real conflict. The purpose of Christ's coming into the world was not to judge but to save. However, judgment is the inevitable result for all who fail to receive Him. The preaching of the gospel has two effects. Those who admit they cannot see are given sight. But those who insist that they can see perfectly, without the Lord Jesus, are confirmed in their blindness.

Some of the Pharisees realized Jesus was speaking of them and of their blindness. They brazenly asked if He was insinuating that they were blind (9:41). "We aren't blind, too, are we?" The answer of the Lord Jesus may be paraphrased as follows: "If you admit yourselves to be blind and sinful and in need of a Savior, then your sins will be forgiven you, and you will be saved. But you profess that you need nothing. You claim that you are righteous and have no sin. Therefore, there is no forgiveness of sins for you." When Jesus said, ". . . you would have no sin," He did not mean that they would be absolutely sinless. But He meant that comparatively speaking, they would be sinless. If they had acknowledged their blindness in failing to recognize Him as Messiah, their sin would have been as nothing compared with the sin of professing to see, yet failing to recognize Him as the Son of God.

## "I Am the Door" (10:1-10)

The Pharisees claimed to be rightful shepherds of the people of Israel. It was to them, in particular, that the Lord Jesus now spoke. The solemn character of what He was about to say is indicated by the expression "Most Assuredly, I say to you."

A sheepfold was an enclosure in which sheep were sheltered at night. It was an area surrounded by a fence and having one opening that was used as a door. The "sheepfold" was the Jewish nation.

Many Jewish people professed to be spiritual rulers and guides. They were self-appointed messiahs for the nation. But they did not come by the door. They did not come the way the Old Testament Scriptures predicted the Messiah would come. They climbed up some other way. They presented themselves to Israel in a manner of their own choosing. These men were not true shepherds, but thieves and robbers. Thieves are those who take what does not belong to them, and robbers are those who use violence in doing so. The Pharisees were thieves and robbers. They sought to rule over the Jews, and yet did everything to hinder them from accepting the true Messiah. They persecuted those who followed Jesus, and eventually they would put Jesus to death.

Verse 2 refers to the Lord Himself. He came to the lost sheep of the house of Israel. He was the true Shepherd. He entered in by the door, that is, He came in exact fulfillment of the Old Testament prophecies concerning the Messiah. He was not a self-appointed Savior, but came in perfect obedience to the will of His Father. He met all the conditions.

In the New Testament sense, a porter was a doorkeeper. There is considerable disagreement as to the identity of the porter in verse 3. Some think this expression refers to the prophets of the Old Testament who foretold the coming of the Christ. Others believe it refers to John the Baptist, since he was the forerunner of the true Shepherd. Others think the doorkeeper is the Holy Spirit who opens the door for the entrance of the Lord into hearts and lives.

The sheep heard the shepherd's voice. They recognized his voice as that of the true shepherd. Just as literal sheep recognize the voice of their own shepherd, so there were those among the Jewish people who recognized the Messiah. Throughout the Gospel, we have heard the Shepherd calling His own sheep by name. He called to several disciples in chapter 1, and they all heard His voice and responded. He called the blind man in chapter 9. The Lord Jesus still calls those who will receive Him as Savior, and the call is personal and individual. The expression "and leads them out" may refer to the fact that the Lord led those who heard His voice out of the sheepfold of Israel. There they were shut up and enclosed. There was no liberty under the law. The Lord leads His sheep into the freedom of His grace. In the last chapter, the Jews had cast the man out of the synagogue. In doing so, they had been assisting the work of the Lord without knowing it!

When the true Shepherd puts forth His sheep, He does not drive them, but He leads them(10:4). He does not ask them to go anywhere that He Himself has not first gone. He is ever out in front of the sheep, their Savior, their Guide, and their Example. Those who are true sheep follow Him. They do not *become* sheep by following His example, but by being born again. But when they are saved, they have a desire to go where He leads. The same instinct that enables a sheep to recognize the voice of the true Shepherd also prompts it to flee from a stranger. The strangers were the Pharisees and other leaders of the Jewish people who were only interested in the sheep for their own personal advantage. The man who received his sight illustrates this. He recognized the voice of the Lord Jesus but knew that the Pharisees were strangers. Therefore, he refused to obey them, even though it meant being excommunicated. It is distinctly stated now that the Lord spoke these words to the Pharisees, but they did not understand—the reason being they were not true sheep. If they had been, they would have heard His voice and would have followed Him.

The Lord, in verse 7, uses a new illustration. He is no longer speaking about the door of the sheepfold, as in verse 2. Now He Himself is the Door of the sheep. It is no longer a question of entering into the sheepfold of Israel. Now the elect sheep of Israel pass out of Judaism and come to Christ, the Door.

We are told in verse 8 that others had come before Christ, claiming authority and position. But the elect sheep of Israel did not hear them because they knew they were claiming what did not rightfully belong to them.

Verse 9 is simple enough for the Sunday School pupil to understand, yet it can never be exhausted by even the most learned scholar. Christ is the Door. Christianity is not a creed, or a church. It is a Person, and that Person is the Lord Jesus Christ. "If anyone enters by Me, he will be saved." Salvation can only be received through Christ. Baptism will not do; neither will the Lord's Supper. We must enter in by Christ, and by the power which He gives. The invitation is for any man. Christ is the Savior of Jew and Gentile alike. But to be saved, a man must enter in. He must receive Christ by faith.

It is a personal act, and without it there is no salvation. Those who do enter in are saved from the penalty, the power, and eventually from the very presence of sin. After salvation, they go in and out. That is, they go into the presence of God by faith to worship, and then they go out into the world to witness for the Lord. It is a picture of perfect liberty in the service of the Lord. Those who enter find pasture. Christ is not only the Savior, and the One who gives freedom, but He is also the Sustainer. His sheep find pasture in the Word of God.

A contrast is presented in verse 10. The thief steals, kills and destroys. He comes to gain his own desires and would even kill the sheep. But the Lord Jesus does not come to the human heart for any selfish reason. He comes to give. He comes that men "might have life, and that they might have it more abundantly." We receive life the moment we accept Him as our Savior. After we are saved there are degrees of enjoyment. The more we turn ourselves over to the Holy Spirit, the more we enjoy the life which has been given to us. We not only have life, we have it more abundantly.

## "I am the Good Shepherd" (10:11-18)

Many times the Lord Jesus used the expression "I am," one of the titles of Deity. Each time He was making a claim to equality with God. Here He presented Himself as the Good Shepherd who laid down His life for the sheep. Ordinarily, the sheep were slain for the shepherd. But the Lord Jesus died for the flock.

"When blood from a victim must flow,  
This Shepherd by pity was led,  
To stand between us and the foe,  
And willingly died in our stead."

In contrast to the Lord Jesus who gave himself for the flock, in verse 12 we read of a hireling; one who was paid for his services. The Pharisees were hirelings. Their interest in the people was prompted by the money they received in return. The hireling did not own the sheep. When danger came, he ran away, and left the sheep to the mercy of the wolves. We do what we do because we are what we are. The hireling was a hireling. He did not love the sheep. Therefore, he was more interested in his own welfare than in their good. There are hirelings in the church today—men who choose the ministry as a comfortable occupation, without true love for God's sheep.

In verse 14, the Lord speaks of Himself as the Good Shepherd. "Good" here means "fair, meet, worthy, choice, excellent." He is all of these. Then He speaks of the intimate relationship that exists between Himself and His sheep. He knows His own, and His own know Him. This is a very wonderful truth.

It is unfortunate that verse 15 appears in the Authorized Version as a new sentence. Actually, it is a part of the preceding verse. We might read as follows: ". . . and I know My sheep, and am known by My own, even as the Father knows Me, and I know the Father." This is truly a thrilling truth! The Lord compared His relationship with the sheep with the relationship that existed between Himself and His Father. The same union, communion, intimacy, and knowledge that there is between the Father and the Son exists between the Shepherd and the sheep. "And I lay down my life for the sheep," He said. Again we have one of the many statements of the Lord Jesus in which He anticipated His death on the cross as a Substitute for sinners.

Verse 16 is the key to the entire chapter. The other sheep to whom the Lord referred were the Gentiles. His coming was especially in connection with the sheep of Israel, but He also had in mind the salvation of Gentiles. The Gentile sheep were not of the Jewish fold. But the great heart of the Lord Jesus went out to these sheep as well, and He was under divine compulsion to bring them to Himself. He knew they would be more ready than the Jewish people to hear His voice. In the latter part of this verse the Authorized Version says, "And there shall be one fold, and one shepherd." However this should read, "And there shall be one flock, and one shepherd." There was a change from the *fold of Judaism* to the *flock of Christianity.* This verse gives a preview of the fact that in Christ, Jew and Gentile would be made one, and that the former distinctions between these peoples would disappear.

In verses 17 and 18 the Lord explained what He would do to bring both Jews and Gentiles to Himself. He would die and would rise again. He spoke of laying down His life and taking it again by His own power. He could only do this because He is God. The Father loved the Lord Jesus because of His willingness to die and rise again, in order that lost sheep might be saved. No one could take the Lord's life from Him. He is God, and thus was greater than all the murderous plots of His creatures. He had power in Himself to lay down His life, and He also had power to take it again. But did not men kill the Lord Jesus? They did. This is clearly stated in Acts 2:23 and in 1

Thessalonians 2:15. The Lord Jesus allowed them to do it, and this was an exhibition of His power to lay down His life. Furthermore, He "gave up the ghost" (John 19:30) as an act of His own strength and will. "This commandment have I received of my Father," He said. The Father had instructed the Lord to lay down His life and to rise again from among the dead. His death and resurrection were an essential part of the Father's will.

## Division among the Jews (10:19-21)

Again the Lord Jesus caused a division among the Jews. Christ's entrance into the world, and into homes, and into hearts, produces a sword, rather than peace. Only when men receive Him as Lord and Savior do they know the peace of God. The Lord Jesus was the only perfect Man who ever lived. He never said a wrong word or committed an evil deed. Yet such is the depravity of man that when He came, speaking words of love and wisdom, men said He had a demon and was mad, and should be ignored. But some thought otherwise. They recognized the words and works of the Lord Jesus as those of a good person and not of a demon.

## Jesus Proved to Be Christ by His Works (10:22-30)

At this point there is a break in the narrative. The Lord Jesus was no longer speaking to the Pharisees, but to the Jews in general. We do not know what time elapsed between verse 21 and verse 22. Incidentally, this is the only mention in the Bible of the feast of the dedication. It is generally believed that this feast was instituted by Judas Maccabeus when the temple was rededicated after being defiled by Antiochus Epiphanes, B.C. 165. It was a yearly feast, instituted by the Jewish people, and not one of the feasts of Jehovah. It was winter—winter actually and spiritually. The public ministry of the Lord Jesus was almost over, and He was about to demonstrate His complete dedication to God the Father by His death on the cross. Verse 24 records a question that is asked of Jesus. Solomon's porch mentioned here was a covered area, adjoining Herod's temple. As the Lord walked there, there would have been plenty of room for the Jews to gather around Him. "How long do You keep us in doubt?" they asked Him. "If You are the Christ, tell us plainly."

In verse 25 Jesus again reminded them of His words and His works. He had often told them that He was the Messiah, and His miracles proved

His claim to be true. Again He reminded the Jews that He performed His miracles by authority of His Father and for His Father's glory. In doing so, He showed that He was indeed the One whom the Father had sent into the world. But their unwillingness to receive Him proved they were not His sheep. If they had been set apart to belong to Him, they would have shown a willingness to believe Him.

Starting in verse 27 Jesus teaches in unmistakable terms that no true sheep of His will ever perish. The eternal security of the believer is a glorious fact. Those who are true sheep of Christ hear His voice. They hear it when the gospel is preached, and they respond by believing on Him. Thereafter, they hear His voice day by day and obey His Word. The Lord Jesus knows His sheep. He knows each one by name. Not one will escape His attention. Not one will be lost through an oversight or carelessness on His part. Christ's sheep follow Him. They recognize the true Shepherd and follow His footsteps.

Christ gives eternal life to His sheep (10:28). This means life that will last forever. It is not life that is conditional on their behavior. It is eternal (everlasting) life. But *eternal* life is also a quality of life. It is the life of the Lord Jesus Himself—a life capable of enjoying the things of God down here, and suitable to heaven itself. Note these next words carefully. *"They shall never perish."* If any sheep of Christ ever perished, then the Lord Jesus would fail to keep a promise, and this is not possible. Jesus Christ is God, and He cannot fail. He has promised that no sheep of His will ever spend eternity in hell.

Does this mean then that a person may be saved and then live the way he pleases? Can he be saved and then carry on in the sinful pleasures of this world? No! In fact, he no longer desires to do these things. He wants to follow the Shepherd. We do not live a Christian life in order to become a Christian or in order to retain our salvation. We live a Christian life because we are Christians. We desire to live a holy life, not out of fear of losing our salvation, but out of gratitude to the One who died for us. The doctrine of eternal security does not encourage careless living, but rather is a strong motive for holy living.

No man is able to pluck a believer out of Christ's hand. His hand is almighty. It created the world; and it even now sustains the world. There is no power that can snatch a sheep from His grasp. Not only is the believer in the hand of Christ, he is in the Father's hand as well. This is a twofold guarantee of safety. God the Father is greater than all, and no one can pluck a believer out of the Father's hand.

In verse 30 the Lord added a further claim to equality with God. "I and My Father are one." Here the thought probably is that Christ and the Father are one in power. Jesus had been speaking about the power that protects the sheep. He added the explanation that His power is the same as the power of God the Father. Of course the same is true of all the other attributes of Deity. The Lord Jesus Christ is God in the fullest sense and is equal with the Father in every way.

## The Jews Try to Stone Jesus (10:31-39)

We see from verse 31 that there was no question in the minds of the Jews as to what the Savior meant. He was setting forth His Deity. They took up stones to kill Him.

Before they had a chance to hurl the stones, the Lord reminded them of the many miracles He had performed by commandment from His Father. He asked which of these good works had so infuriated them that they wanted to kill Him. The Jews denied that it was for any of His miracles that they sought to slay Him. They wanted to stone Him because He had spoken blasphemy by claiming to be equal with God the Father. They refused to admit He was anything more than a man, yet He made Himself God as far as His claims were concerned. They would not tolerate this.

In verse 34 Jesus quoted to the Jews from Psalm 82:6. He called this a part of their law. In other words, it was taken from the Old Testament Scriptures which they acknowledged to be the inspired Word of God. The complete verse is as follows: "I said, You are gods; and all of you are children of the most High." The Psalm was addressed to the judges of Israel. They were called "gods" not because they were actually divine, but because they represented God when they judged the people. The Hebrew word for "gods" and "judges" is the same. It could also be translated "mighty ones." (It is clear from the rest of the Psalm that they were only men and not deities, because they judged unjustly, showed respect of persons, and otherwise perverted justice.) The Lord used this verse from the Psalms to show that God used the word "gods" to describe men to whom the Word of God came. In other words, these men were spokesmen for God. Jehovah spoke to the nation of Israel through them. "They manifested God in His place of authority and judgment, and were the powers whom God had ordained."

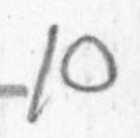

"And the scripture cannot be broken," said the Lord, expressing His belief in the inspiration of the Old Testament Scriptures. To Him they were infallible writings which must be fulfilled, and which cannot be denied. In fact, the very words of Scripture are inspired, not just its thoughts or ideas. His whole argument is based on the single word "gods."

The Lord was arguing from the lesser to the greater in verse 36. If unjust judges were called "gods" in the Old Testament, how much more right did He have to say He was the Son of God. The word of God *came* to them; He *was* and *is* the Word of God. They were *called* gods; He *was* and *is* God. It could never have been said of them that the Father had sanctified them and sent them into the world. They were born into the world like all other sons of fallen Adam. But Jesus was sanctified by God the Father from all eternity to be the Savior of the world, and He was sent into the world from heaven where He had always dwelt with His Father. Thus Jesus had every right to claim equality with God. He was not blaspheming when He claimed to be the Son of God, equal with the Father. The Jews themselves used the term "gods" to apply to corrupt men who were mere spokesmen or judges for God. How much more could He claim the title because He actually *was* and *is* God.

In verse 37 the Savior appealed to the miracles which He performed as proof of His divine commission. However, note the expression "the works of my Father." Miracles, in themselves, are not a proof of deity. We read in the Bible of evil beings having the power at times to perform miracles. But the miracles of the Lord were the works of His Father. They proved Him to be the Messiah in a twofold way. They were the miracles which the Old Testament Scriptures predicted would be performed by the Messiah. They were miracles of mercy and compassion, works that benefited mankind and which would not be performed by an evil person.

Verse 38 has been helpfully paraphrased as follows: "If I do the works of my Father, then, though ye may not be convinced by what I say, be convinced by what I do. Though ye resist the evidence of my words, yield to the evidence of my works. In this way learn to know and believe that I and my Father are indeed one, He in me and I in Him, and that in claiming to be His Son, I speak no blasphemy." Again the Jews realized that instead of denying His previous claims, the Lord Jesus had only strengthened them. Therefore they made another attempt to arrest Him, but He eluded them once more. The time was not far distant now when He would permit Himself to be taken by them, but as yet, His hour had not come.

## Jesus Escapes Across the Jordan (10:40-42)

The Lord went now to the very place beyond the Jordan where He began His public ministry (10:40). His three years of wondrous words and mighty works were drawing to a close. He ended them where He began them—outside the established order of Judaism, in a place of rejection and loneliness. Many now came to Him and those who came to Him were probably sincere believers. They were willing to bear His reproach, to take their place with Him outside the camp of Israel. These followers paid a glowing tribute to John the Baptist. They remembered that John's ministry was not spectacular or sensational, but it was true. Everything he said about the Lord Jesus was fulfilled in the ministry of the Savior. This should encourage each one who is a Christian. We may not be able to do mighty miracles or gain public attention, but at least we can bear a true testimony to our Lord and Savior Jesus Christ. This is of great value in God's sight.

It is lovely to notice that in spite of His rejection by the nation of Israel, the Lord did find some lowly, receptive hearts. "Many," we are told, "believed on him there." Thus it is in every age. There is always a remnant of the people who are willing to take their place with the Lord Jesus, cast out by the world, hated and scorned, but enjoying the sweet fellowship of the Son of God.

CHAPTER

# 8

# The Raising of Lazarus (John 11–12)

## The Sickness of Lazarus (11:1-4)

We now come to the last miracle in the *public* ministry of the Lord Jesus as recorded by John. In some senses, it was the greatest of all—the raising of a dead man. Lazarus lived in the little village of Bethany, just about two miles east of Jerusalem. Bethany was also known as the home of Mary and her sister Martha. Pink's comment is interesting: "The presence of God's elect children is the one thing which makes towns and countries famous in God's sight. The village of Martha and Mary is noticed, while Memphis and Thebes are not named in the New Testament." John explains in verse 2 that it was Mary of Bethany who had anointed the Lord Jesus with ointment and wiped His feet with her hair. This singular act of devotion was emphasized by the Holy Spirit. The Lord loves the willing affection of His people.

The Lord was apparently on the east side of the Jordan River when Lazarus took sick. The sisters immediately sent Him word that Lazarus, whom He loved, was sick. They appealed to His love for their brother as a special reason why He should come and help.

"This sickness is not to death," Jesus said in verse 4. He did not mean that Lazarus would not die but that death would not be the final outcome of this sickness. The real purpose of the sickness was "the glory of God, that the Son of God may be glorified through it." God allowed this to happen so

Jesus would come and raise Lazarus from the dead and thus be manifested again as the true Messiah. Men would glorify God for this mighty miracle. There is no suggestion that Lazarus' sickness was a result of some special sin in his life. On the contrary, he is presented as a devoted disciple and as a special object of the Savior's love.

## The Journey of Christ to Bethany (11:5-16)

When sickness enters our homes, we are not to conclude that God is displeased with us. Here sickness was directly linked with His love. We would naturally think that if the Lord really loved these three believers, then He would hurry to their home. Instead, when He heard the news, He remained two days where He was. God's delays are not God's denials. If our prayers are not answered immediately, perhaps He is teaching us to wait, and if we wait patiently, we will find that He will answer our prayers in a much more marvelous way than we anticipated. Not even the Lord's love for Martha and Mary and Lazarus could force Him to act ahead of the proper time. Everything He did was in obedience to His Father's will and in keeping with the divine plan. Then, after two seemingly wasted days, the Lord Jesus proposed to the disciples that they should all go into Judea once more.

In verse 8 we see that the disciples were still painfully aware of how the Jews had sought to kill Christ after He had given sight to the blind man. They expressed surprise that He would even think of going into Judea in the face of such personal danger. The Lord answered them as follows. There are twelve hours of light in a day, when men can work. As long as a man works during this allotted time, there is no danger of his stumbling or falling because he can see where he is going and what he is doing. The light keeps him from accidental death through stumbling. The spiritual meaning is as follows. Jesus was walking in obedience to the will of God. There was thus no danger of His being killed before the appointed time. He would be preserved until His work was done. In a sense this is true of every believer. "We are immortal until our work is done." If we are walking in fellowship with the Lord and doing His will, there is no power on earth that can kill us before God's time. In contrast, the man who walks in the night is one who is not faithful to God, but is living in self-will. This man stumbles easily because he does not have divine guidance to illuminate his way.

In verse 11 the Lord spoke of Lazarus' death as sleep. In the New Testament sleep is *never* applied to the soul, only to the body. The believer's *soul* goes to be with Christ, which is far better. The Lord Jesus revealed His omniscience in this statement. He knew Lazarus was already dead, although the report He had heard was that Lazarus was sick. He knew because He is God. He was going to awaken Lazarus. While any man may awaken another out of physical sleep, only the Lord could awaken Lazarus out of death. Here Jesus expressed His intention of doing that very thing.

The disciples did not understand the Lord's reference to sleep. In verse 12 they said, in effect, "If Lazarus is sleeping, he will recover." Perhaps they believed sleeping to be a symptom of recovery and concluded that if Lazarus was able to sleep soundly then he had passed the crisis and would get well. The verse might also mean that if physical sleep were the only thing wrong with Lazarus, then there was no need to go to Bethany to help him. It is possible the disciples were fearful for their own safety and seized upon this excuse for not going to Bethany. It is now clearly stated that when the Lord Jesus spoke of sleep, He was referring to death but that His disciples had not understood this. There could now be no misunderstanding. The Lord told His disciples plainly that Lazarus was dead. How calmly the disciples received the news! They did not ask the Lord, "How do You know?" He spoke with complete authority, and they did not question His knowledge.

The Lord Jesus was not glad that Lazarus had died but in verse 15 we read that He was glad He was not at Bethany at the time. Had He been there, Lazarus would not have died. Nowhere is it recorded in the New Testament that a person died in the presence of the Lord. The disciples would see a greater miracle than the prevention of death. They would see a man raised from the dead. In this way, their faith would be strengthened. Therefore, the Lord Jesus said that He was glad for their sakes that He had not been at Bethany. "To the intent ye may believe," He added. The Lord was not implying that the disciples had not already believed on Him. Of course they had! But the miracle they were about to see would greatly strengthen their faith in Him. Therefore, He urged them to go with Him.

Verse 16 gives us insight into the disciple Thomas. He reasoned that if the Lord Jesus went to Bethany, He would be killed by the Jews. If the disciples went with Jesus, they too would be killed. And so in a spirit of pessimism and gloom, he urged them all to go with Jesus. His words are not an example of great faith or courage, but of discouragement.

## "I am the Resurrection and the Life" (11:17-27)

The fact of Lazarus' being in the grave for four days was added as proof that he was dead. Notice how the Holy Spirit safeguards the fact that the resurrection of Lazarus was a miracle.

Bethany was about two miles east of the city of Jerusalem. Its nearness to Jerusalem made it possible for many of the Jews to visit Mary and Martha, and to comfort them. Little did they realize that in a short time their comfort would no longer be needed. This house of mourning would be turned into a house of great joy.

We see in verse 20 that as soon as Martha heard that Jesus was approaching she ran out to meet Him. The meeting took place just outside the village. We are not told why Mary remained in the house. Perhaps she had not received the report of Jesus' arrival. Maybe she was paralyzed by grief. Or was she simply waiting in a spirit of prayer and trust? Did she sense what was about to happen because of her closeness to the Lord? We do not know.

It was real faith that enabled Martha to believe that Jesus could have prevented Lazarus from dying (11:21). Still, her faith was imperfect. She thought He could only do this if He were bodily present. She did not realize He could heal from a distance, still less that He could raise the dead. Often in times of sorrow, we talk like Martha. We think that if such and such a drug or medicine had been discovered, then this loved one would not have died. But all these things are in the hands of the Lord, and nothing happens to one of His own without His permission. Again Martha's faith shone out. She did not know *how* the Lord Jesus would help, but she believed He would. She had confidence that God would grant Him His request and that He would bring good out of this seeming tragedy. But she did not dare to believe her brother would be raised from the dead. The word Martha used for "ask" is the word normally used to describe a creature supplicating the Creator. Obviously Martha did not recognize the deity of the Lord Jesus. She realized that He was a great and unusual Man, but probably no greater than the prophets of old. To lift her faith to greater heights, Jesus made the startling announcement that Lazarus would rise again. The Lord Jesus dealt tenderly with this sorrowing woman to lead her step by step to faith in Him as the Son of God. Martha knew that Lazarus would rise from the dead some day, but she had no thought that it could happen right then and there.

She believed in the resurrection of the dead and believed it would happen in what she called "the last day." In reply the Lord said in effect, "You do not understand Me, Martha. I do not mean that Lazarus will rise again at the last day. I am God, and I have the power of resurrection and of life. I can and will raise Lazarus from the dead right now."

Then the Lord looked forward to the time when all believers will be raised, the time when He comes back to take His people home (11;25). At that time there will be two classes of believers. There will be (1) those who have died in faith, and (2) those who are living at His return. He comes to the first as the *Resurrection* and to the second as the *Life.* The first are described in the latter part of verse 25—"He that believes in me, though he were dead, yet shall he live." Those believers who have died before Christ's coming will be raised from the dead. The second class is described in verse 26. Those who are alive at the time of the Savior's coming and who believe on Him will never die. They will be changed, in a moment, in a twinkling of an eye, and taken home to heaven with those who have been raised from the dead. What precious truths have come to us as a result of Lazarus' death! God brings sweetness out of bitterness and gives beauty for ashes. Then the Lord pointedly asked Martha, to test her faith, "Do you believe this?" Martha's faith blazed out in noontime splendor. She confessed Jesus to be the Christ, the Son of God, whom the prophets had predicted would come into the world. And notice she made this confession *before* Jesus had raised her brother from the dead!

## Jesus Weeps at the Grave (11:28-37)

Immediately after this confession, Martha rushed back to the village and greeted Mary with the breathless announcement, "The Teacher has come and is calling for you." The Creator of the universe and the Savior of the world had come to Bethany and was calling for Mary. And it is still the same today. This same wonderful Person stands and calls men to Him in the words of the gospel. Each one is invited to open the door of his heart and to let the Savior in. Mary's response was immediate. She rose quickly and went to Jesus (11:29).

Now Jesus met Martha and Mary outside the village of Bethany. The Jews did not know He was near since Martha's announcement of the fact to Mary had been a secret one. It was not unnatural that they should conclude that Mary had gone out to the grave to weep there.

Mary fell down at the Savior's feet. It may have been an act of worship, or it may be she was simply overcome with grief. Like Martha, she uttered the regret that Jesus had not been present in Bethany, for in that case, Lazarus would not have died. To see Mary and her friends in sorrow caused Jesus to groan and to be troubled. Doubtless He thought of all the sadness, suffering, and death which had come into the world as a result of man's sin. This caused Him inward grief. He asked where Lazarus was buried. The Lord of course knew, but He asked the question to awaken expectation to encourage faith, and to call forth man's cooperation.

Verse 35 is the shortest in the English Bible. It records one of three instances where the Lord is said to have wept. (He wept also in sorrow over the city of Jerusalem and He wept in the garden of Gethsemane.) That Jesus wept evidenced His true humanity. He shed tears of grief when He witnessed the effects of sin on the human race. The fact that Jesus wept in the presence of death shows it is not improper for Christians to weep when their loved ones are taken. However, Christians do not sorrow as others who have no hope.

The Jews saw in the tears of Jesus proof of His love for Lazarus (11:36). They were correct. But He also loved them just as much though many of them failed to understand this. Again the Lord Jesus caused questionings among the people. Some recognized Him as the same One who had given sight to the blind man. They wondered why He could not have prevented Lazarus from dying. Of course, He could have done so, but instead He was going to perform a mightier miracle.

## The Seventh Sign: The Raising of Lazarus (11:38-44)

The Lord was filled with inward heaviness. It would seem that Lazarus' grave was a cave under the earth, into which one would have to descend by a ladder or a flight of stairs. A stone was placed on top of the cave. Verse 39 records that Jesus commanded the onlookers to remove the stone from the grave. He could have done this Himself by merely speaking the word. However, God does not ordinarily do for men what they can do for themselves. Martha expressed horror at the thought of opening the grave. Her brother's body had been there for four days and had begun to decompose! Apparently no attempt had been made to embalm the body of Lazarus. He would have been buried the same day he died as was the custom. The fact that Lazarus was in the grave for four days is important. He was certainly not asleep or in a coma. All the Jews knew he was dead. His resurrection can only be explained as a miracle.

It is not clear when the Lord Jesus had spoken the words of verse 40. In verse 23 He had told her that her brother would rise again. What He here said presumably was the substance of what He had previously told her. Notice the order in this verse. "Believe . . . see." It is as if the Lord Jesus had said, "If you will just believe, you will see Me perform a miracle that only God could perform. You will see the glory of God revealed in Me. But first you must believe, and then you will see."

In verse 41, the stone was then removed from the grave. Before performing the miracle Jesus thanked His Father for having heard His prayer. No previous prayer of the Lord Jesus is recorded in this chapter. But doubtless He had been speaking to His Father continually during this entire period and had prayed that God's Name might be glorified in the resurrection of Lazarus. Here He thanked the Father in anticipation of the event. He prayed audibly so that the people might understand that the Father had sent Him, that the Father told Him what to do and what to say, and that He always acted in dependence upon God. Here again we have the essential union of God the Father and the Lord Jesus Christ emphasized.

Verse 43 records one of the few instances in the New Testament where Jesus is said to have cried with a loud voice. It has been suggested that if He had not mentioned Lazarus by name, then all the dead in the graves would have come forth! How did Lazarus come forth? Some think he hobbled out of the grave; others think that he crawled out on hands and knees; still others point out that with his body wrapped tightly in grave clothes it would have been impossible for him to have come out by his own power. They suggest that his body came out of the grave through the air until his feet touched the ground in front of the Lord Jesus. The fact that his face was bound about with a napkin is further proof that he had been dead. No one could have lived for four days with his face bound with a cloth. The Lord commanded the people to loose Lazarus and to let him go. "He alone can raise the dead, but to us He gives the task of removing stones of stumbling, and of unwinding the bands of prejudice and superstition."

## The Jews Take Action Against the Lord (11:45-57)

To many of the onlookers, this miracle unmistakably proclaimed the deity of the Lord Jesus Christ, and they believed on Him. Who else but God could call forth a dead body from the grave? But the effect of a miracle on a person's life depends on his moral condition. If a man's heart is evil, rebellious, and unbelieving, he will not believe even though he should see one raised from the dead. That was the case we see in verse 46. Some of the Jews who witnessed the miracle were unwilling to accept the Lord Jesus as their Messiah. They went to the Pharisees to report what had happened in Bethany. Why? Probably that the Pharisees might be further stirred up against the Lord and seek to put Him to death.

The chief priests and Pharisees gathered together to discuss what action should be taken. "What are we going to do about this?" they said. "Why are we so slow in acting? This man is performing many miracles, and we are doing nothing to stop him." The Jewish leaders spoke these words to their own condemnation. They admitted Jesus was performing many miracles. Why then did they not believe on Him? They did not want to believe because they preferred their sins to the Savior. It has been well said, "This is a marvelous admission. Even our Lord's worst enemies confess that our Lord did miracles, and many miracles. Can we doubt that they would have denied the truth of His miracles if they could? But they do not seem to have attempted it. They were too many, too public, and too thoroughly witnessed for them to dare to deny them. How, in the face of this fact, modern infidels and skeptics can talk of our Lord's miracles as being impostures and delusions, they would do well to explain! If the Pharisees who lived in our Lord's time, and who moved heaven and earth to oppose His progress, never dared to dispute the fact that He worked miracles, it is absurd to begin denying His miracles now, after eighteen centuries have passed away."

In verse 48 we see that the Jews felt they could no longer remain inactive. If they did not intervene, the mass of the people would be persuaded by the miracles of Jesus. If the people acknowledged Jesus to be King, it would mean trouble with Rome. The Romans would think that Jesus had come to overthrow their empire; they would move in and punish the Jews. The expression "take away both our place and nation" means that the Romans would destroy the temple and scatter the Jewish people. These very things took place in A.D. 70, not, however, because the Jews accepted the Lord, but because they rejected Him. F. B. Meyer says, "Christianity endangers businesses, undermines profitable but wicked trades, steals away customers from the devil's shrines, attacks vested interests, and turns the world upside down. It is a tiresome, annoying, profit-destroying thing."

Caiaphas was high priest from A.D. 26–36. He presided at the religious trial of the Lord and was present when Peter and John were brought before the Sanhedrin in Acts 4:6. He was not a believer of the Lord Jesus, in spite of the words which he here uttered. The chief priests and Pharisees, he argued, were wrong in thinking the Jews would die on account of Jesus. Jesus would die for the Jewish nation. It was expedient that Jesus should die for the people, so that the whole nation would not perish. Why, it sounds as if Caiaphas really understood the reason for Jesus' coming into the world. We would almost think he had accepted Jesus as the Substitute for sinners! But no! What he said was true, but he himself did not believe on Jesus to the saving of his soul (11:51). He did not speak "of himself," that is, he did not make up these things by himself. He did not speak this of his own will. The message he uttered was given him by God. It was a prophecy that Jesus would die for the nation of Israel. It was given to Caiaphas because he was high priest that year. God spoke through him because of the office he held and not because of his own personal righteousness, for he was a sinful man. The prophecy of Caiaphas, contained in verse 52, was not only that the Lord Jesus would die for Israel. He would also gather together His elect among the Gentiles of the earth. Some think Caiaphas was referring to Jewish people scattered abroad throughout the earth, but more probably he was referring to Gentiles who would believe on Christ through the preaching of the gospel.

The Pharisees were not convinced by the miracle at Bethany. They were the more hostile than ever. In verse 53 we read that from that day forth, they plotted His death with new intensity. Realizing the mounting hostility of the Jews, Jesus went off to a city called Ephraim. We do not know where Ephraim was except that it was in a quiet, secluded area near the wilderness.

The announcement now made that the Jews' Passover was at hand reminds us we are coming to the close of the Lord's public ministry (11:55). It was at this very Passover He was to be crucified. Prior to the Passover, the people were required to go to Jerusalem to purify themselves. For instance, if a Jew had touched a dead body, he must go through a certain ritual to be cleansed from his ceremonial defilement. This purifying was done through various types of washings and offerings. The Jewish people were thus seeking to purify themselves, while at the same time they were planning the death of the Passover Lamb. What a terrible exposure of the wickedness of the heart of man!

As the people gathered in Jerusalem, they began to think about the miracle worker named Jesus. Would He come to the feast? The question "What do you think—that He will not come to the feast?" might better be broken down into two questions as follows: "What do you think? Surely he will not come to the feast." They knew official orders had gone out from the chief priests and the Pharisees for the arrest of Jesus. Any Jew who knew of His whereabouts was commanded to notify the authorities so that He might be taken and put to death.

## Mary Anoints the Feet of Jesus (12:1-8)

The home in Bethany was a place where Jesus loved to be. There He enjoyed sweet fellowship with Lazarus, Mary, and Martha. In coming to Bethany at this time, he was exposing Himself to danger because nearby Jerusalem was headquarters for all the forces that were arrayed against Him.

In spite of the many opposed to Jesus, there were a few who were true to Him. Lazarus, who sat at the table with the Lord Jesus, was one of those. Martha served. The Scripture does not say anything about what Lazarus saw or heard from the time he died until he was raised again.

Several instances are recorded in the Gospels where Jesus was anointed by a woman. No two incidents are exactly alike, and it is not necessary to suppose that this anointing by Mary is recorded in any of the other Gospels. Mary's devotion to Christ caused her to take this pound of very costly ointment and anoint His feet (12:3). She was saying in effect that nothing was too valuable to give to Him. He is worthy of everything that we have and are.

Each time we meet Mary she is at the feet of Jesus. Here she is wiping His feet with her hair. A woman's hair is her glory so she was laying her glory, as it were, at His feet. Needless to say, Mary would have carried the fragrance of the ointment for some time after this. Thus when Christ is worshipped, the worshippers themselves carry away something of the fragrance of that moment. No house is so filled with pleasant odor as the house where Jesus is given His rightful place.

In verse 4 the flesh is seen intruding into this most sacred of occasions. Judas could not stand to see precious ointment used in this way. He did not consider the Lord to be worth three hundred pence. He felt the ointment should have been sold and given to the poor. This was sheer hypocrisy. He cared no more for the poor than he did for Jesus. He was about to betray the Lord, not for three hundred pence, but for a tenth of that amount. Someone has summarized it in this way, "That anyone could follow Christ as a disciple for three years, see all His miracles, hear all His teaching, receive at His hand repeated kindnesses, be counted an apostle, and yet prove rotten at heart in the end, all this at first sight appears incredible and impossible! Yet the case of Judas shows plainly that the thing can be. Few things, perhaps, are so little realized as the extent of the fall of man." John is quick to add that Judas did not protest this "waste" because he loved the poor, but because he was a thief. He carried the bag for the disciples as their treasurer and took care of their finances, such as they were.

The Lord answered in verse 7, "Do not prevent her from doing this. She has kept this ointment for the day of My burial. Now she wants to lavish it on Me in an act of affection and worship. She should be permitted to do so." There would never be a time when there would not be poor people on whom others might lavish their kindness. But the Lord's ministry on earth was swiftly drawing to a close. Mary would not always have the opportunity to minister to Him. Surely this should remind us that spiritual opportunities are passing. We should never delay doing what we can for the Savior.

## Plot Against Lazarus (12:9-11)

The word quickly spread that Jesus was near Jerusalem. It was no longer possible to keep His presence secret. Many Jews came to Bethany to see Him, and others came to see Lazarus, whom He had raised from the dead.

So insane is the hatred of the human heart, the chief priests plotted the death of Lazarus. One would think he had committed high treason by being raised from the dead! They considered him worthy of death because through him many people believed on Jesus. Lazarus was therefore an enemy to the Jewish cause, and he must be put out of the way. Those who bring others to the Lord are always made the target for persecution and even martyrdom.

## Christ's Entry into Jerusalem (12:12-19)

We now come to the triumphal entry of Jesus into Jerusalem. It was the Sunday before His crucifixion. It is difficult to know exactly what the crowds thought about Jesus. Did they really understand He was the Son of God and the Messiah of Israel? Or did they merely look upon Him as a King who would deliver them from Roman oppression? Were they carried away with the emotion of the hour? Doubtless some in the group were true believers, but the general impression is that most of the people had no real heart interest in the Lord. The palm branches they waved are a token of rest and of peace after sorrow (Revelation 7:9). The word "Hosanna" means "Save now, we pray you." Thus it would seem that the people were acknowledging Jesus to be the One sent from God to save them from Roman cruelty and to give them rest and peace after the sorrow of their long years of Gentile oppression.

Jesus entered the city riding on a young ass (12:14). The ass of course was a common beast of burden, but more than that, the Lord Jesus was fulfilling prophecy. John quoted from Zechariah 9:9 to prove this—"Fear not, daughter of Zion: behold, your King comes, sitting on an ass's colt." "The daughter of Zion" is a figurative reference to the Jewish people, Zion being a hill in the city of Jerusalem. The disciples did not realize that what was happening was an exact fulfillment of Zechariah's prophecy, that Jesus was actually entering Jerusalem as the rightful King of Israel. But after the Lord had gone back to heaven to be glorified at the right hand of the Father, it dawned on them that these events were a fulfillment of the Scriptures.

In verses 17 and 18 tell us more about the crowd. In the crowd that watched Jesus enter Jerusalem were many who had seen Him raise Lazarus from the dead. These told the others about that amazing miracle. As the report spread, a great throng of people came forth to meet Jesus. Unfortunately, their motive was curiosity rather than true faith. As the crowd grew in size, and interest in the Savior mounted, the Pharisees were beside themselves (12:19). Nothing they could say or do had the slightest effect. With a sweeping gesture they cried out that the whole world had gone after Him. They did not realize that the interest of the crowd was but a passing thing, and that those who truly worshipped Jesus as the Son of God were really very few.

## The Greeks Desire to See Jesus (12:20-26)

The Greeks who came to Jesus at this time were Gentiles who had become converts to Judaism. They had come to worship at the feast for they no longer followed the religious practices of their ancestors. Their coming to the Lord Jesus pictured the time when, the Jews having rejected the Lord Jesus, the Gentiles would hear the gospel and many of them believe. No reason is given why they came to Philip. Perhaps his Greek name and the fact that he was of Bethsaida of Galilee made him attractive to the Gentile proselytes. Their request in verse 21 was noble indeed. "Sir," they said, "we wish to see Jesus." No one with this desire is ever turned away. Perhaps Philip was not too sure whether the Lord would see these Greeks. Christ had previously told the disciples not to go to the Gentiles with the gospel, so Philip went to Andrew, and together they went to Jesus.

The Lord's answer in verse 23, at first seems irrelevant to the request of the Greeks. Some have suggested that since the Greeks, as a nation, were interested in self-culture, self-advancement, and self-enjoyment, Jesus told them their philosophy was directly opposed to the law of harvest. Others suggest that the Lord was saying the only way He could give these Greeks the blessings which they sought was by going to the cross and dying for them. Seed never produces grain until it has fallen into the ground and died. The Lord here referred to Himself in verse 24 as a corn (or kernel) of wheat. If He did not die, He would abide alone. He would enjoy the glories of heaven by Himself; there would be no saved sinners there to share His glory. But if He died, He would provide a way of salvation by which many might be saved.

The same applies to us as T. G. Ragland says: "If we refuse to be corns of wheat—falling into the ground, and dying; if we will neither sacrifice prospects, nor risk character, and property, and health; nor, when we are called, relinquish home, and break family ties, for Christ's sake; *then we shall abide alone.* But if we wish to be fruitful, we must follow our Blessed Lord Himself, by becoming a corn of wheat, and dying, *then we shall bring forth much fruit.*"

The Lord continues in verse 25 and tells us that many people think the important things in life are food, clothing, and pleasure. They live for these things. They fail to realize the soul is more important than the body and by neglecting their soul's welfare, they lose their lives. On the other hand, there are those who count all things loss for Christ. To serve Him they forego things highly prized among men. These are the people who keep their lives unto life eternal. To hate one's life means to love Christ more than one loves his own interests. To serve Christ, one must follow Him. His servants must obey His teachings and resemble Him morally (12:26). They must apply the example of His death to themselves. He promises throughout His constant presence and protection, not only in the present life but throughout eternity as well. Service now will receive God's approval in a coming day. Whatever one suffers of shame or reproach here will seem small indeed when compared with the glory of being publicly commended by God the Father in heaven.

## Christ Faces His Approaching Death (12:27-36)

Increasingly now the Lord's thoughts were on soon coming events. He was thinking of the cross and contemplating the time when He would become the Sin Bearer. Thinking of the hour of His crucifixion, His soul was troubled. How should He pray in such a moment? Should He ask His Father to save Him from the hour? No! For this purpose He had come into the world and was going to the cross. He was born to die. So He prayed that the Name of His Father might be glorified. He was more interested that honor should come to God than in His own comfort or safety. God now spoke from heaven, saying He *had* glorified His Name and would glorify it again. The Name of God had been glorified by the earthly ministry of Jesus. The thirty silent years in Nazareth, the three years of public ministry, the wonderful words and works of the Savior—all of these glorified the Name of the Father. But still greater glory would be brought to God through the death, burial, resurrection and ascension of Christ.

We read in verse 29 that some of those standing by mistook the voice of God for thunder. Some people are always trying to put a natural explanation on spiritual things. Men who are unwilling to accept the fact of miracles try to explain the miracles away by some natural law. Others knew it was not thunder, and yet they did not recognize it as the voice of God. Realizing it must have been superhuman, they could only conclude that it was the voice of an angel. God's voice can only be heard and understood by those who are helped by the Holy Spirit. Men can listen to the gospel over and over, and yet it remains meaningless to them unless the Holy Spirit speaks to them through it. The Lord explained to the listeners that the voice did not need to be audible in order for Him to hear it. It was made audible for the sake of those who were standing by.

"Now is the judgment of this world," He said in verse 31. The world was about to crucify the Lord of life and glory. In doing so, it would condemn itself. Sentence would be passed upon it for its awful rejection of Christ. Condemnation was about to be passed on guilty mankind. The prince of this world is Satan. Satan was utterly defeated at Calvary. He thought he had succeeded in doing away with the Lord Jesus. Instead, the Savior provided a way of salvation for men, and at the same time He defeated Satan and all his hosts. The sentence of doom has not been carried out on the devil as yet, but his doom has been sealed, and it is just a matter of time before he will be cast into the lake of fire.

The first part of verse 32 refers to Christ's death on the cross. He was nailed to a cross of wood and lifted up from the earth. If He were thus crucified, the Lord said, He would draw all men to Him. Some think Christ draws all men either to salvation or to judgment. Others think if Christ is lifted up in the preaching of the gospel, then there will be a great power in the message, and souls will be drawn to Him. Probably the correct explanation is that the crucifixion of the Lord Jesus has resulted in all kinds of men being drawn to Him. It does not mean all men without exception, but men from every nation, tribe, and language.

Verse 33 explains that when the Lord Jesus spoke of being lifted up, He signified the kind of a death He would die, namely, death by crucifixion. Here again we have evidence of the all-knowledge of the Lord. He knew in advance He would be nailed to a cross. The people were puzzled by this statement of the Lord about being lifted up. They knew He claimed to be the Messiah, and yet they knew from the Old Testament that the Messiah would live forever (see Isaiah 9:7; Psalm 110:4; Daniel 7:14; Micah 4:7). Notice the people quoted Jesus as saying, "The *Son of man* must be lifted up." Actually, He had said, "*I*, if *I* be lifted up from the earth." Of course, the Lord had referred to Himself many times as the Son of man, so it was not difficult for the people to put the two thoughts together.

The people asked Jesus who the Son of man was. In reply He spoke of Himself as the Light of the world (12:35). He reminded them the Light would be with them only for a short while. They should come to the Light and walk in the Light; otherwise darkness would come upon them, and they would stumble about in ignorance. The Lord was apparently likening Himself to the sun and the daylight it offers. The sun rises in the morning, reaches its peak at noon, and descends over the horizon in the evening. It is only with us for a limited number of hours. We should avail ourselves of it while it is here, because when the night comes, we do not have the benefit of it. The one who believes on the Lord Jesus is the one who walks in the light. The one who rejects Him walks in darkness and does not know where he is going. He lacks divine guidance, and stumbles through life. Again the Lord Jesus warned His listeners to believe on Him while there was still opportunity (12:36). Then they would become children of the Light and be assured of direction through life and into eternity. After speaking these words, the Lord departed from the people and remained in obscurity for a while.

## Failure of the Jews to Believe (12:37-43)

John now expresses amazement that, though Jesus had performed so many mighty works, yet the people did not believe on Him. Their unbelief was not caused by lack of evidence. The Lord had given the most convincing proofs of His deity, but the people did not want to believe. They wanted a king to rule over them, but they did not want to repent. This unbelief was a fulfillment of Isaiah 53:1. The question, "Lord, who has believed our report?" calls for the answer, "Not many." The arm of the Lord speaks of the mighty power of God revealed only to those who believe the report concerning the Christ. Because not many accepted the announcement concerning the Messiah, the power of God was not revealed to many.

It was not God's fault that they could not believe. The Lord Jesus presented Himself to Israel and the nation rejected Him. Over and over again, He came back with the offer of salvation, but they kept saying "no" to Him. The more men reject the gospel, the harder it becomes for them to receive it. God causes them to be smitten with "judicial blindness," that is, a blindness which is God's judgment upon them for refusing His Son. In verse 40 John quoted from Isaiah 6:9, 10. God blinded the eyes of the people of Israel and hardened their hearts—not at first, but only after they had closed their own eyes and hardened their own hearts. As a result they cut themselves off from sight, understanding, conversion, and healing. The quotation is from the memorable chapter in which Isaiah saw the glory of God. John explains that it was Christ's glory Isaiah saw, and it was of Christ that he spoke. Thus, verse 41 is another link in the chain of evidence that proves Jesus to be God.

It might seem strange to us but we read in verse 42 that many of the chief rulers of the Jews became intellectually convinced that Jesus was the Messiah, but they did not dare to share their conviction with the others lest they be excommunicated. Perhaps these men were genuine believers in the Lord Jesus, but it is extremely doubtful. Where there is true faith, there will be confession of Christ, sooner or later. When Christ is really accepted as Lord, one makes it known, regardless of the consequences. These men were more interested in the approval of their fellows than in the approval of God. They thought more of man's praise than of God's. Can a person like this really be a genuine believer in Christ? See chapter 5, verse 44, for the answer.

## The Peril of Unbelief (12:44-50)

Let us paraphrase verse 44—"The one who believes on Me actually believes not only on Me, but also on My Father who sent Me." Here again the Lord taught His absolute union with the Father. It was impossible to believe on one, without believing on the other. To believe on Christ is to believe on God the Father. One cannot believe on the Father unless he gives equal honor to the Son. In one sense, no man can see God the Father. He is Spirit, and therefore invisible. But Jesus came to show us what God is like, not physically, of course, but morally. He has revealed to us the character of God. Therefore, whoever has seen Christ has seen God the Father.

The illustration of light was apparently one of the Lord's favorites. Here in verse 46, He again referred to Himself as a Light coming into the world that those who believe on Him should not remain in darkness. Apart from Christ, men are in deepest darkness. They do not have a right understanding of life, death, or eternity. But those who come to Christ in faith no longer grope about for the truth, because they have found the truth in Him. The purpose of Christ's coming was not to condemn but to save. He did not sit in judgment on those who refused to hear His words or to believe on Him. This does not mean that He will not judge these unbelievers in a coming day, but that judgment was not the object of His first advent. So far as the coming judgment day is concerned, those who refuse His words will stand before God and the words, the teaching, of the Lord will be sufficient to condemn them. "I have not spoken on My own authority," He said in verse 49. The things He taught were not things He had made up Himself or learned in the schools of men. He had spoken those things the Father commissioned Him to speak. This is what will condemn men at the last day. The word Jesus spoke was the Word of God, and men refused to hear it. The Father had told Him not only what to say but what He should speak. There is a difference. The expression "what I should say" refers to the substance of the message. The words "what I should speak" refer to the very words which the Lord Jesus used in teaching the truth of God. Jesus knew the Father had commissioned Him to give everlasting life to those who would believe on Him. Therefore, He delivered the message as it was given Him by the Father.

CHAPTER

# 9

# In the Upper Room (John 13–14)

We now come to a distinct break in the narrative. Up to this point the Lord has presented Himself to Israel. Seven distinct signs or miracles have been recorded, each one illustrating an experience that will result when a sinner puts his faith in Christ. The signs are:

1. The changing of the water into wine (2:1-12). This pictures the sinner as a stranger to divine joy being transformed by the power of Christ.
2. The healing of the nobleman's son (4:46-54). This pictures the sinner as sick and in need of spiritual health.
3. The healing of the cripple at the pool of Bethesda (chapter 5). The sinner is without strength, helpless and unable to do a thing to remedy his condition. The Lord Jesus cures him of his infirmity.
4. The feeding of the five thousand (chapter 6). The sinner is without food, hungry and in need of that which imparts strength. The Lord Jesus provides food for his soul so that he never needs to hunger.
5. The calming of the Sea of Galilee (6:16-21). The sinner is in a place of danger. The Lord Jesus rescues him from the storm.
6. The healing of a man blind from birth (chapter 9). This pictures man's spiritual blindness until touched by the power of Christ. Man cannot see his own sinfulness, or the beauties of the Savior, until he is enlightened by the Holy Spirit.
7. The raising of Lazarus from the dead. The sinner is dead in trespasses and in sins and needs life from above.

All of these signs prove Jesus to be the Christ, the Son of God.

In chapter 13 the Upper Room Discourse begins. Jesus is now no longer walking among the hostile Jews. He has retired with His disciples to an upper room in Jerusalem for a final time of fellowship with them before going forth to His trial and crucifixion. The portion from chapter 13 through chapter 17 is one of the best loved sections in the entire New Testament.

## Jesus Washes His Disciples' Feet (13:1-11)

The day before the crucifixion has come. The Lord knew the time had come for Him to die, to rise again, and to go back to heaven. He had loved His own, that is, those who were true believers. He loved them to the end of His earthly ministry, and will continue to love them throughout eternity. He loved them to an infinite degree, as He was about to demonstrate.

The expression "supper being ended" in verse 2 is not accurate. It should be "during supper" or "when the supper was taking place." The Bible does not say which supper is referred to here—whether the Passover, the Lord's Supper, or an ordinary meal. During supper Satan sowed the thought in Judas' mind that the time was ripe to betray Jesus. Judas had plotted against the Lord long before this, but he was now given the signal for carrying out his evil plans.

Jesus was conscious of His deity. He knew the work that had been committed to Him; He knew that He had come from God the Father and that He was returning to Him (13:4). Conscious of who He was, of His mission and of His destiny, He stooped down and washed the disciples' feet. Rising from supper, He laid aside the long outer garment He was wearing and He put a towel around Himself as an apron, taking the place of a slave. The Lord who left the palaces above had come as a Servant, to minister to those He had created.

The open sandals, so common in eastern lands, made it necessary to wash one's feet frequently. It was common courtesy for a host to have a slave wash the feet of his guests. Here the divine Host became the slave and performed this lowly service. "Jesus at the feet of the traitor—what a picture in verse 6! What lessons for us!" Peter was shocked. He expressed disapproval that One as great as the Lord should condescend to one as unworthy as he. Jesus now taught Peter that there was a spiritual meaning to what He was doing. Foot-washing was a picture of spiritual washing.

Peter knew the Lord was performing the physical act, but he did not realize the spiritual significance. He would know it soon, however, for the Lord explained it. And he would know it by experience when later he was restored to the Lord after having denied Him.

Peter illustrates the extremes of human nature. In verse 8 he vowed that the Lord would never wash his feet—and "never" means "not for eternity." The Lord answered Peter that apart from His washing, there could be no fellowship with Him. The meaning of foot-washing is now unfolded. As Christians walk through this world, they become defiled. Listening to vile talk, looking at unholy things, working with ungodly men inevitably defile the believer. He needs to be constantly cleansed.

This cleansing takes place through the water of the Word. We read and study the Bible, we hear it preached, we discuss it one with another, and it cleanses us. If we neglect the Bible, these wicked influences remain in our minds and lives defiling us and rendering us insensitive to sin. Jesus said to Peter "you have no part with me," that is fellowship with the Lord can remain unhindered only by the continual cleansing action of the Scriptures.

Now in verse 9 Peter shifted to the other extreme. A minute ago, he said, "Never." Now he said, "Wash me all over." In His reply, the Lord Jesus used two different words for "wash." What He really said was this: "He who is bathed needs only to wash his feet, but is completely clean." There is a difference between the bath and the basin. The *bath* speaks of the cleansing we receive at the time of salvation. Cleansing from the *penalty* of sin through the blood of Christ takes place only once. The *basin* speaks of cleansing from the *pollution* of sin and must take place continually through the Word of God. There is one bath but many foot cleansings. "You are clean, but not all of you," added the Lord. The disciples had received the bath of regeneration—that is, all but Judas. He had never been saved. Knowing all things, the Lord knew Judas would betray Him, so He singled out one as never having had the bath of redemption.

## Christ Teaches the Disciples to Follow His Example (13:12-20)

It would seem that Christ washed the feet of *all* the disciples. Then He put on His outer garments and sat down to explain the spiritual meaning of what He had done. He opened the conversation by asking a question. The questions of the Savior make an interesting study. They form one of His most common methods of teaching. The disciples had acknowledged Jesus to be their Teacher and Lord, and they were right in doing so. If the Teacher and Lord had washed the disciples' feet, what excuse could they have for not washing one another's feet? Did the Lord mean they should literally wash each other's feet with water? Was He here instituting an ordinance for the church? No, the meaning here was spiritual. They should keep each other clean by constant fellowship over the Word. If one sees his brother growing cold or worldly, he should lovingly exhort him from the Bible.

Verse 15 tells us that the Lord had given them an object lesson, an example of what they should do to one another spiritually. If pride or personal animosities prevent us from stooping to serve our brethren, we should remember that we are not greater than the Lord. He humbled Himself to wash those who were unworthy and unthankful, and He knew that one of them would betray Him. Would you minister in a lowly way to a man you knew was about to betray you for money? Those who were sent (the disciples) should not consider themselves too lofty to do anything that the One who sent them (the Lord Jesus) had done. To know these truths concerning humility, unselfishness and service is one thing. The real value and blessedness lie in doing them.

What the Lord had just been teaching about service did not apply to Judas (13:18). He was not one of those whom the Lord would send into all the world with the gospel. Jesus knew the Scriptures concerning His betrayal must be fulfilled—such Scriptures as Psalm 41:9. Judas was one who had eaten his meals with the Lord for three years, and yet he "lifted up his heel" against Him—an expression indicating that he betrayed the Lord. In Psalm 41, the betrayer is described by the Lord as "mine own familiar friend." The Lord revealed His betrayal to the disciples in advance so that when it came to pass, they would recognize Deity. The word "he" should be omitted from verse 19. "You may believe that I AM." The Jesus of the New Testament is the Jehovah of the Old Testament. Thus fulfilled prophecy is one of the great proofs of the deity of Christ and also, we might add, of the inspiration of the Scriptures.

In verse 20, because the Lord knew His betrayal might cause the disciples to stumble or doubt, He added a word of encouragement. They should remember they were being sent on a divine mission. They were to be so closely identified with Him that to receive *them* was the same as receiving *Him.* Also, those who received Christ received God the Father.

## The Lord Foretells That Judas Would Betray Him (13:21-30)

The knowledge that one of His disciples would betray Him caused the Lord to be deeply stirred. It seems that Jesus was here giving the betrayer a final opportunity to abandon his plan. Without exposing him directly, the Lord revealed His knowledge that one of the twelve would betray Him. But even this did not change the betrayer's mind. The disciples did not suspect Judas. They were surprised that one of their number would do such a thing and puzzled as to who he could be. The words "perplexed about whom he spoke" mean "uncertain of whom he spoke."

In those days, people did not sit up at a table for a meal but reclined on low couches. The "disciple whom Jesus loved" was John, the writer of this Gospel (13:23). He does not mention his name, but does mention the special affection the Savior had for him. The Lord loved all the disciples, but John enjoyed a special sense of closeness to Him. Peter probably used some kind of sign rather than speaking audibly. Perhaps by nodding with his head, he asked John to find out the name of the betrayer. In verse 25 we see John leaning back on the Savior's breast and asking the fateful question. Probably he spoke in a whisper and was answered in a low tone as well.

Jesus said He would give the sop (KJV) or piece of bread dipped in wine or meat juice to the traitor (13:26). Some say that an Eastern host gave the sop to the honored guest at a meal. By making Judas the honored guest, the Lord thus tried to win him to repentance by His grace and love. Others suggest that the sop was commonly passed in this way in connection with the Passover supper. If so, then evidently Judas left during the Passover supper and before the Lord's Supper was instituted.

The devil had already put it into Judas' heart to betray the Lord. Now we read in verse 27 that Satan entered into him. At first, it was a suggestion but Judas entertained it, liked it, and agreed to it. Now the devil took control of him. Knowing the betrayer was now fully determined, the Lord told him to do it quickly. Obviously He was not encouraging him to do evil but expressing sorrowful resignation.

Verse 28 confirms the fact that the conversation between Jesus and John about the sop was not heard by the other disciples. They still did not know that Judas was about to betray their Lord. Some of them thought Jesus was telling Judas to go quickly and buy something for the feast. Others thought that, because Judas was the treasurer, the Savior had instructed him to make a donation to the poor. Judas received the sop and then left the Lord and the disciples. The Scriptures add the meaningful words "and it was night." It was night not only in a literal sense, but it was night spiritually for Judas—a night of gloom and remorse that would never end. It is always night when men turn their backs on the Savior.

## A New Commandment Is Given (13:31-35)

As soon as Judas left, the Lord began to speak with the disciples more freely and more intimately. The tension was gone. "Now the Son of Man is glorified," He said. The Lord was anticipating the work of redemption He was about to accomplish. His death might have seemed like defeat, yet it was the means whereby lost sinners might be saved. It was followed by His resurrection and ascension, and He was greatly honored in it all. "And God is glorified in Him." The work of the Savior brought great glory to God. It proclaimed Him to be a holy God who could not pass over sin, but also a loving God who did not desire the death of the sinner; it proclaimed how He could be a just God, yet be able to justify sinners. Every attribute of deity was superlatively magnified at Calvary. Verse 32 starts, "If God is glorified in Him." The "if" here does not express any doubt. It means "since." "Since God is glorified in him." "God will also glorify Him in Himself," God will see that appropriate honor is given to His beloved Son. "And glorify Him immediately." He will do it without delay. The Father fulfilled this prediction by raising the Lord Jesus from the dead and seating Him at His own right hand in heaven. He would not wait until the kingdom was ushered in. He would glorify His Son immediately.

For the first time in John' Gospel the Lord addressed His disciples as little children—a term of endearment (13:33). And He used it only after Judas had departed. He was only to be with them for a little while. Then He would die on the cross. They would seek Him then, but would not be able to follow Him, for He would return to heaven. The Lord had told the same thing to the Jews, but He meant it in a different sense. For the disciples, His departure would only be temporary. He would come again for them (chapter 14). But for the Jews, His leaving would be final. He was returning to heaven, and they could not follow Him because of their unbelief.

During His absence, the disciples were to be governed by the commandment of love (13:34). This commandment was not new inasmuch as the Ten Commandments taught love to God and to one's neighbor, but it was new in other ways. It was new because Jesus had given a living demonstration of it and because the Holy Spirit would empower believers to obey it. It was new in its superiority to the old; the old said, "Love your neighbor," but the new said, "Love your enemies." It was new because it called for a higher degree of love: "As I have loved you, that you also love one another." It has been well said, "The law of love to others 'was now to be explained with new clearness, enforced by new motives and obligations, illustrated by a new example, and obeyed in a new manner.'"

Verse 35 summarizes a true mark of Christian discipleship as love for fellow Christians. This requires divine power, and this power is given only to those indwelt by the Spirit.

## Peter's Denial of Christ Foretold (13:36-38)

From verse 36 we see Peter did not understand that Jesus had spoken of His death. He thought He was going on some earthly journey and did not understand why he could not go along. The Lord told Peter he would follow later, that is, when he died, but could not do so now. With typical devotion and enthusiasm, Peter expressed in verse 37, willingness to die for the Lord. He thought he could endure martyrdom by his own strength. Later he did die for the Lord, but only because he had been given special strength and courage by God. The Lord checked Peter's "zeal without knowledge" by telling him that before the night was ended, he would deny the Lord three times. Thus Peter was reminded of his weakness and cowardice, and his inability to follow the Lord for even a few hours by his own power.

## "I Am the Way, the Truth, and the Life" (14: 1-14)

Some link the first verse of chapter 14 to the last verse of the previous chapter and think it was spoken to Peter. He would deny the Lord, but there was comfort for him. But it was probably spoken to all the disciples, and we should understand a pause after the last chapter. The thought seems to be this: "I am going away, and you will not be able to see me. But do not let your heart be troubled. You believe in God, and yet you do not see Him. Now believe in Me in the same way." Here is another important claim to equality with God. In verse 2 the Father's house refers to heaven where there are many dwelling places. There is room there for all the redeemed.

If it were not so, the Lord would have said so; He would not have them build on false hopes. "I go to prepare a place for you," He said. This may have two meanings. The Lord Jesus went to Calvary to prepare a place for His own. It is through His atoning death that believers are assured of a place in heaven. But also the Lord went back to heaven to prepare a place. We do not know very much about that place, but we know provision is being made for every child of God. A prepared place for a prepared people!

Verse 3 refers to the time when the Lord will come in the air, when those who have died in faith will be raised, when the living will be changed, and when all the blood-bought throng will be taken home to heaven (1 Thessalonians 4:13-18; 1 Corinthians 15:51-58). This is a personal, literal coming of Christ. As surely as He went away, He will come again. His desire is to have His own with Him for all eternity.

A more accurate translation of verse 4 is: "And where I go, you know the way." He was going to heaven, and they knew the way to heaven for He had told them many times. Apparently Thomas did not understand the meaning of the Lord's words. Like Peter, he may have been thinking of a journey to some place on the earth. Jesus explained that He Himself is the Way to heaven. He does not merely show the way; He is the Way. Salvation is in a Person. Accept that Person as your own and you have salvation. Christianity is Christ. The Lord is the Truth. He is not just One who teaches the truth; He is the Truth. He is the embodiment of Truth. Those who have Christ have the Truth. It is not found anywhere else. Christ Jesus is the Life. He is the source of life, both spiritual and eternal. Those who receive Him have eternal life because He is the Life. Jesus is not just one of many ways. He is the *only* Way. No man comes to the Father but by Him. The way to God is not by the Ten Commandments, not by the Golden Rule, not by ordinances, not by church membership— it is by Christ and Christ alone. Many say that it does not matter what a person believes as long as he is sincere. They say all religions have some good in them and they all lead to heaven at last. But Jesus said, "No man cometh unto the Father but by me."

Once more, in verse 7, the Lord emphasized the mysterious union that exists between the Father and Himself. Had the disciples recognized who Jesus really was, they would have known the Father also, because the Lord revealed the Father to men. From now on, and especially after Christ's resurrection, the disciples would understand that Jesus was God the Son. Then they would realize that to know Christ was to know the Father, and to see the Lord Jesus was to see God. This verse does not teach that God and the Lord Jesus are the same Person. There are three distinct Persons in the Godhead, but there is only one God.

Philip, in verse 8, wanted the Lord to give some special revelation of the Father, and that would be all he would ask. He did not understand that everything the Lord was, and did, and said was a revelation of the Father.

The Lord in verse 9 patiently corrected him. Philip had been with the Lord for a long time. He was one of the first disciples to be called (John 1:43). Yet the full truth of Christ's deity and of His unity with the Father had not yet dawned upon him. He did not know that when he looked at Jesus, he was looking upon One who perfectly displayed the Father. The Lord's words "I am in the Father, and the Father in me" describe the closeness of the union between the Father and the Son. They are separate Persons, yet They are one as to attributes and will. We should not be discouraged if we cannot understand this. No mortal mind will ever understand the Godhead. We must give God credit for knowing things we can never know. If we fully understood Him, we would be as great as He! Some words must be supplied in the latter part of this verse to complete the meaning. We might paraphrase it as follows: "The words that I speak unto you, I do not speak by My own authority, but the Father who dwells in Me, He speaks the words; and the works that I do, I do not do them on My own initiative, but the Father who dwells in Me, He performs these miracles." The Lord had power to speak the words and to do the miracles, but He came into the world as the Servant of Jehovah, and He spoke and acted in perfect obedience to the Father. The disciples should believe that He was one with the Father because of His own testimony to that fact. But if not, then they should certainly believe because of the miracles He performed.

The Lord in verse 12 then predicted that those who believe on Him would perform miracles like He did, and even greater miracles. In the book of Acts, we read of the apostles performing miracles of bodily healing, similar to those of the Savior. But we also read of greater miracles—such as the conversion of three thousand on the day of Pentecost. It was to the world-wide proclamation of the gospel, the salvation of many souls, and the building of the Church that the Lord referred by the expression "greater works." It is greater to save souls than to heal bodies. When the Lord returned to heaven, He was glorified, and the Holy Spirit was sent to earth. It was through the power of the Holy Spirit that the apostles performed these greater miracles.

What a comfort it must have been to the disciples to know that, even though the Lord was leaving them, they could pray to the Father in His Name and receive their requests (14:13). This verse does not mean that a believer can get anything he wants from God. The key to the promise is in the words "in my name." "Whatever you ask in My name." To ask In Jesus' Name is not simply to insert His Name at the end of the prayer. It is to ask in accordance with His mind and will. It is to ask for those things that will glorify God, bless mankind, and be for our own spiritual good. In order to ask in Christ's Name, we must live in close fellowship with Him. Otherwise we would not know His attitude. The closer we are to Him, the more our desires will be the same as His are. The Father is glorified in the Son because the Son only desires those things that are pleasing in God's sight. As prayers of this nature are presented and granted, it causes great glory to be brought to God. The promise is repeated for emphasis and as a strong encouragement to God's people. Live in the center of His will, walk in fellowship with the Lord, ask for those things that the Lord would desire, and your prayers will be answered.

## The Promise of the Comforter (14:15-26)

The Lord Jesus was about to leave the disciples, and they would be filled with sorrow. They should express their love to Him by keeping His commandments. Not by tears, but by obedience. The commandments of the Lord are the instructions that He has given us in the Gospels, as well as all the other writings of the New Testament.

It is interesting to note in verse 16 that when the word "pray" is used of the Lord, it is not the word sometimes used to describe an inferior praying to a superior. It is the word that describes one making request of his equal. The Lord would pray the Father to send another Comforter. The word "Comforter" means one who comes to the side of another to help. It is also translated Advocate. The Lord Jesus is our Advocate or Comforter, and the Holy Spirit is another Comforter— not another of a different kind, but another of similar nature. The Holy Spirit would abide with believers forever. In the Old Testament, the Holy Spirit came upon men at various times, but often left them. Now it would no longer be so. He would come to remain forever.

The Holy Spirit is called the Spirit of truth because His teaching is true and He glorifies Christ who is the truth (14:17). The world cannot receive the Holy Spirit because it cannot see Him. Unbelievers want to see before they will believe. The unsaved do not know or understand the Holy Spirit.

He may convict them of sin, and yet they do not know that it is He. The disciples knew the Holy Spirit. They had known His work in their own lives, and had seen Him working through the Lord Jesus. "He dwells with you, and shall be in you," said Jesus. Before Pentecost, the Holy Spirit came upon men and dwelt with them. But since Pentecost, when a man believes on the Lord Jesus, the Holy Spirit takes up His abode in that man's life forever. The prayer of David, "Take not thy Holy Spirit from me," would not be suitable today. The Holy Spirit is never taken from a believer, although He might be grieved, and quenched, and hindered.

The Lord would not leave His disciples as orphans, or desolate (14:18). He would come again to them. He came, of course, after His resurrection, but it is doubtful if that is what is meant. In another sense, He came to them in the Person of the Holy Spirit on the day of Pentecost. In a third sense, He will come to them again in a literal manner at the end of this age, when He will take His chosen ones home to heaven.

No unbeliever saw the Lord Jesus after His burial (14:19). After He was raised, He was seen only by those who loved Him. But even after His ascension, His disciples continued to see Him by faith. This is doubtless meant by the words "but you see me" or rather "you will see me." "Because I live, you will live also," added the Lord. Here He was looking forward to His resurrection life that would be the pledge of life for all who trusted Him. Even should they die, they would be raised again to die no more. The expression "at that day" in verse 20 probably refers again to the descent of the Holy Spirit. He instructs us that just as there was a vital link between the Son and the Father, so there would be a marvelous union of life and interests between Christ and His saints. It is difficult to explain how Christ is in the believer, and the believer is in Christ at the same time. A poker can be in the fire and the fire in the poker, but this does not tell the full story. Christ is in the believer in the sense that His life is communicated to him. He actually dwells in the believer through the Holy Spirit. The believer is in Christ in the sense that he stands before God in all the merit of the Person and work of Christ.

In verse 21 we see that the real proof of one's love to the Lord is obedience to His commandments. The Father loves such. In one sense, the Father loves all the world. But He has a special love for those who love His Son. Those are also loved by Christ, and He makes Himself known to them in a special way. The more we love the Savior, the better we shall know Him.

It was the misfortune of the Judas mentioned in verse 22 to have the same name as the traitor. But the Spirit of God kindly distinguished him from Iscariot. This might have been the man who wrote the book of Jude. He could not understand how the Lord could appear to the disciples without also being seen by the world. Doubtless he thought of the Savior's coming as a conquering King. He did not understand that the Lord would manifest Himself to His own in a spiritual manner. They would see Him by faith through the Word of God. By the Spirit of God we can actually know Christ better today than the disciples knew Him when He was on earth. Those in the front of the crowd were closer to Him than those in the rear. But today, by faith, each of us can enjoy the closest of fellowship with Him.

If a person truly loves the Lord, he will want to obey all of His teachings, not just isolated commandments (14:23). The Father loves those who are willing to obey His Son without questions or reservations. Both Father and Son are especially near to such loving and obedient hearts. On the other hand, those who do not love Him do not keep His sayings. And they are not only refusing the words of Christ, but those of God the Father as well (14:24).

While He was with them, our Lord taught His disciples up to a certain point but He could not reveal more truth to them because they could not take it in (14:25). But the Holy Ghost (i.e., the Holy Spirit) would reveal more. The Spirit was sent by the Father in the Name of Christ on the day of Pentecost. He came to represent Christ's interests on earth. He did not come to glorify Himself but to draw men and women to the Savior. "He shall teach you all things," said the Lord. He did this first of all through the spoken ministry of the apostles; then through the written New Testament. The Holy Spirit would bring to remembrance all the Savior had taught. The Lord presented in germ form all the teaching that is developed by the Holy Spirit in the rest of the New Testament.

## Jesus Leaves His Peace to the Disciples (14:27-31)

A person about to die usually writes a last will and testament in which he leaves his possessions to his loved ones. Here the Lord Jesus was doing that very thing. However, He did not bequeath material things but something that money could not buy—PEACE, inward peace of conscience that arises from a sense of pardoned sin and of reconciliation with God. Christ can give it because He purchased it with His own blood at Calvary. It is not given as the world gives—sparingly, selfishly, and for a short time. His gift of peace is forever. Why then should a Christian be troubled or afraid?

Jesus had already told the disciples He was going to leave them, and then return later to take them to heaven. If they loved Him, He said, this would cause them to rejoice (14:28). Of course, in a sense they did love Him. But they did not fully appreciate who He was, and thus their love was not as great as it should have been. "You would rejoice because I said, I am going to the Father, for My Father is greater than I." At first it seems as if this verse contradicts all that Jesus had taught concerning His equality with God the Father. But there is no contradiction, and the passage explains the meaning. When the Lord Jesus was here upon earth, He was hated and hunted, persecuted and pursued. Men blasphemed Him, reviled Him, and spat on Him. He endured terrible indignities from the hands of His creatures. The Father never suffered such rude treatment from men. He dwelt in heaven, far away from the wickedness of sinners. When the Lord returned to heaven, He would be where indignities could never come. Therefore, the disciples should rejoice when He said that He was going to the Father, because in this sense the Father was greater than He. The Father was not greater *as God,* but greater because He never came into the world as Man to be cruelly treated. As far as the attributes of deity are concerned, the Son and the Father are equal. But when we think of the lowly place which the Lord Jesus took as a Man here on earth, we realize that in that sense, God the Father was greater than He. In unselfish concern for the fearful disciples, the Lord revealed these future events to them so that they would not be offended, disheartened or afraid.

From verse 30 we see the Lord knew that the time for His betrayal was drawing near and that He would not have much more time to talk with His own. Satan was coming, but the Savior knew the enemy could find no taint of sin in Him.

We might paraphrase verse 31 as follows: "The time of my betrayal is at hand. I shall go voluntarily to the cross. This is the Father's will for me. It will tell the world how much I love my Father. That is why I am now going without offering any resistance." With this, the Lord bade the disciples to arise and go with Him. It is not clear whether they moved from the upper room at this point. Perhaps the rest of the discourse took place as they walked along.

C H A P T E R

# 10

# Talks Along the Way (John 15–17)

## "I am the True Vine" (15:1-11)

In the Old Testament, the nation of Israel was depicted as a vine planted by Jehovah. The nation, however, had proved unfaithful and unfruitful so the Lord Jesus, in verse 1, now presented Himself as the true Vine. God the Father is the Husbandman (i.e., the Farmer, or here, the One who cares for the vineyard). Opinions differ as to what is meant by the fruitless branch in verse 2. Some think it is a false professor who pretends to be a Christian but has never really been united to Christ by faith. Others think it is a true Christian who loses his salvation because of his failure to bear fruit. This is clearly impossible because it contradicts so many other passages which teach that the believer has an eternal salvation. Others think that it is a true Christian who becomes a backslider. He gets away from the Lord and becomes interested in the things of this world. He fails to manifest the fruit of the Spirit—love, joy, peace, longsuffering, gentleness, goodness, faith, meekness, temperance. As a result, the Lord chastens him with sickness, sorrow, or, in extreme cases, He removes him from the world because of his poor testimony. We favor this latter view.

The branch that bears fruit is the Christian who is growing more like the Lord Jesus. Even such vines need to be purged or cleansed. Just as a real vine must be cleansed from insects, mildew, and fungus, so a Christian must be cleansed from worldly things that cling to him (15:3). The cleansing agent is the Word of the Lord. The disciples had originally been cleansed by the Word at the time of their conversion. Furthermore even as the Savior had been talking to them, His Word had had a purifying effect on their lives. Thus, this verse may refer to justification and sanctification.

In verse 4 the words "to abide" mean to stay where you are. The Christian has been placed in Christ; that is his position. In daily walk, he should stay in intimate fellowship with the Lord. A branch abides in a vine by drawing all its life and nourishment from the vine. So we abide in Christ by spending time in prayer, reading His Word, fellowshipping with His people, and being continually conscious of our union with Him. As we thus maintain constant contact with Him, we are conscious of His abiding in us and supplying us with spiritual strength and resources. The branch can only bear fruit as it abides in the vine. The only way believers can bear the fruit of a Christ-like character is by living in touch with Christ.

Christ Himself is the Vine; believers are the branches (15:5). It is not a question of the branch living its life for the Vine, but simply of letting the life of the Vine flow out through the branches. Sometimes we pray, "Lord, help me to live my life for You." It would be better to pray, "Lord Jesus, live out Your life through me." Without Christ, we can do nothing. A vine branch has one great purpose—to bear fruit. It is useless for making furniture or for building homes. It does not even make good firewood. But it is good for fruit bearing—as long as it abides in the vine.

Verse 6 has caused much difference of opinion. Many believe that the person described is a believer who falls into sin and is subsequently lost. Such an interpretation is in direct contradiction to the many Scriptures which teach that no true child of God will ever perish. Others believe that this person is a professor—one who pretends to be a Christian but who was never born again. Judas is often used as an illustration. Perhaps this is the proper meaning. We would like to suggest that this man is a true believer for it is with true Christians that this section is concerned. The subject, however, is not salvation but abiding and fruit bearing. This man, through carelessness and prayerlessness, gets out of touch with the Lord. As a result, he commits some sin, and his testimony is ruined. Through failure to abide in Christ, he is cast forth as a branch—not by Christ, but by men. *Men* gather the branches and cast them into the fire, and they are burned. It is not God who does it, or angels, but men. What does this mean? It means that men scoff at this backslidden Christian. They drag his name in the mud. They throw his testimony as a Christian in the fire. This is illustrated in the life of David. He was a true believer, but he became cold in heart toward the Lord and committed the sins of adultery and murder. He caused the enemies of the Lord to blaspheme. Even today atheists ridicule the name of David (and of David's God). They cast him, as it were, into the fire.

Verse 7 tells us that the abiding life is the secret of a successful prayer life. The closer we get to the Lord, the more we will learn to think His thoughts after Him. The more we get to know Him through His Word, the more we will understand His will. The more our will agrees with His, the more we can be sure of having our prayers answered. Children of God exhibit the likeness of Christ to the world and the Father is honored (15:8). People are forced to confess He must be a great God when He can transform such wicked sinners into such godly saints. Notice the progression in this chapter: fruit (v. 2), more fruit (v. 2), much fruit (v. 8). "So you will be My disciples." This can hardly mean that we become disciples by abiding in Christ; the way to become a disciple is to believe on the Lord Jesus. It means we are *manifest* as His disciples when we abide in Him. Others can then see that we are true disciples, that we resemble our Lord.

The love which the Savior has for us is the same as the love of the Father for the Son (15:9). Our hearts are made to bow in worship when we read such words. The love is the same in quality and in degree. It is a vast, wide, deep, unmeasurable love, that passes knowledge, and can never be fully comprehended by man. "Abide in My love," said Jesus in verse 9. We should continue to realize His love and to enjoy it in our lives. The first part of verse 10 tells how we can continue (or abide) in His love; it is by keeping His commandments. The second half of the verse sets before us our Perfect Example. The Lord Jesus kept His Father's commandments. Everything He did was in obedience to the will of God. He remained in the constant enjoyment of the Father's love. Nothing came in to mar that sweet sense of loving fellowship.

Jesus found His own deep joy in communion with God His Father (15:11). He wanted His disciples to have that joy that comes from dependence upon Him. He wanted His joy to be theirs. Man's idea of joy is to be as happy as he can, leaving God out of his life. The Lord taught that real joy comes by taking God into one's life as much as possible. "That your joy may be full," or better, "fulfilled." Their joy would be fulfilled in abiding in Christ and in keeping His commandments. Many have used John 15 to teach doubts concerning the security of the believer. But the Lord's purpose was not "that your doubts might be fulfilled," but "that your joy might be fulfilled."

## Disciples Commanded to Love One Another (15:12-17)

The Lord was soon to leave His disciples. They would be left in a hostile world. As tensions increased, there would be the danger of the disciples' contending with one another. So, in verse 12, the Lord leaves this standing order, "Love one another, as I have loved you." They should be willing to die for one another (15:13). People who are willing to do this do not fight with each other. The greatest example of human self-sacrifice is for a man to die for his friends. Believers are called to this type of devotion. Some lay down their lives in a literal sense; others spend their whole lives in untiring service for the people of God. The Lord Jesus is the Example. He laid down His life for His friends. Of course, we are enemies by natural birth, but when we are saved we become His friends. So it is correct to say He died for His friends as well as for His enemies. We show we are His friends by keeping His commandments (15:14). This is not the way we become His friends, but the way we exhibit this to the world.

The Lord in verse 15 now emphasized the difference between a servant and a friend. A servant is simply expected to do work marked out for him, but a friend is taken into one's confidence. To a friend we reveal our plans for the future. Confidential information is shared with him. In one sense the disciples would always continue to be servants of the Lord, but they would be more than this—they would be friends. The Lord was even now revealing to them the things which He had heard from His Father. He was telling them of His own departure, the coming of the Holy Spirit, His own coming again, and their responsibility to Him in the meantime. Someone has pointed out that as branches, we receive (v. 5); as disciples, we follow (v. 8); and as friends, we commune (v. 15).

Lest there should be any tendency for the disciples to become discouraged and give up, the Lord reminded them in verse 16 that He was the One who had chosen them. He chose them to eternal salvation, to discipleship, and to fruitfulness. In the King James Version of verse 16 part f it reads "And ordained you." This had nothing to do with ordination as it is practiced today by men. It referred to the appointment by Christ, and it had to do with the work which lay before the disciples. We are to "bear fruit." Fruit may mean the graces of the Christian life, such as love, joy, peace. Or it may mean souls won for the Lord Jesus Christ. There is a close link between the two. It is only as we are manifesting the first kind of fruit that we will ever be able to bring forth the second. The expression "that your fruit should remain" implies that fruit here means the salvation of souls. The Lord had chosen the disciples to go and bring forth lasting fruit. He was not interested in mere professions of faith in Himself, but in genuine cases of salvation. L. S. Chafer notes that in this chapter we have prayer effectual (v. 7); joy celestial (v. 11); fruit perpetual (v. 16). "That whatever you ask . . ." The secret of effective service is prayer. The disciples were sent forth with the guarantee that the Father would grant them whatever they asked in Christ's Name.

The Lord was about to warn the disciples about the enmity of the world. He began as we have seen by telling them in verse 17 to love one another, to stick together, and to stand unitedly against the foe.

## The Hatred of the World Predicted (15:18-27)

The disciples were not to be surprised or disheartened if the world hated them (15:18). (The "if " does not express any doubt that this would happen; it was certain.) The world hated the Lord, and it will hate all who resemble Him. Men of the world love those who live as they do—those who use vile language and who indulge in the lusts of the flesh. A Christian condemns them by his holy life, and so they hate him. The word "servant" in verse 20 means "slave," and "lord" means "master." The disciple should not expect any better treatment from the world than his Lord received. He will be persecuted just as Christ was. His word will be refused just as the Savior's was.

This hatred and persecution is "for my name's sake." It is because the believer is linked to Christ; because he has been separated from the world by Christ; and because he bears Christ's Name and likeness. The world is ignorant of God. They do not know that the Father sent the Lord into the world to be the Savior. But ignorance is no excuse.

The Lord was not teaching in verse 22 that if He had not come, then men would not have been sinners. From the time of Adam, all men had been sinners. But their sin would not have been nearly so great as it now was. These men had seen the Son of God and heard His wonderful words. They could find no fault in Him whatever. Yet they rejected Him. It was this that made their sin so great. Thus it was a matter of comparison. Compared with their terrible sin of rejecting the Lord of glory, their other sins were as nothing. Now they had no excuse for their sin. We are reminded in verse 23 that they had rejected the Light of the world. In hating Christ, they had hated the Father. The two are one. They could not say that they loved God, for if they had, they would have loved Him whom God sent.

They were not only responsible for having heard the teaching of Christ, they also saw His miracles (15:24). This added to their condemnation. They saw miracles that no other man had ever performed. To reject Christ in face of this evidence was inexcusable. All their other sins were minor compared to this. The Lord compared all their other sins to this one sin, and said that the former were as nothing when placed alongside the latter. Because they hated the Son, they hated the Father, and this was their terrible condemnation. The Lord realized that man's attitude toward Him was in exact fulfillment of prophecy. In Psalm 69:4, it was predicted that Christ would be hated without any reason. Now that it had happened, the Lord commented that the very Old Testament Scriptures which these men prized had predicted their hatred of Him. The fact that it was prophesied did not mean that these men had to hate Christ. They hated Him by their own deliberate choice, but God foresaw that it would happen, and He caused David to write it in advance.

In spite of man's rejection, there would be a continued testimony to Christ. It would be carried on by the Comforter—the Holy Spirit. Here the Lord said He would send the Comforter from the Father (15:26). In John 14:16, the Father was the One who sent the Spirit. This is another proof of the equality of the Son and the Father. The Spirit of truth proceeded from the Father. This meant that He was constantly being sent forth by God, and His coming at the day of Pentecost was a special instance of this. The Spirit testifies concerning Christ. This is His great mission. He does not seek to occupy men with Himself, though He is a member of the Trinity. He directs the attention of both sinner and saint to the Lord of glory. The Spirit would witness directly through the disciples. They had been with the Lord from the beginning of His public ministry and were especially qualified to tell of His Person and work. If anyone could have found any imperfection in the Lord, those who had been with Him most could have. But they never knew Him to commit a sin of any kind. They could testify to the fact that He was the sinless Son of God and the Savior of the world.

## Persecution Foretold (16:1-4)

The disciples cherished the hope of the Jewish people generally—that the Messiah would set up His kingdom and that the power of Rome would be broken. Instead of that, the Lord told them He was going to die, rise again, and go back to heaven. The Holy Spirit would come, and the disciples would go out as witnesses for Christ. They would be hated and persecuted. We find in verse 1 that the Lord told them all this in advance so they would not be disillusioned, offended, or shocked.

In verse 2 the lord continues to tell the disciples what is ahead for them. Excommunication from the synagogue was considered by most Jews to be one of the worst things that could happen. Yet this would happen to these Jews who were disciples of Jesus. The Christian faith would be so hated that those who sought to stamp it out would think they were pleasing God. This shows how a person may be very sincere, and very zealous, and yet be very wrong. Failure to recognize the deity of Christ would be at the root of the matter. The Jews would not receive Him, and thus refused to receive the Father. Again the Lord warned the disciples in advance so they would not be moved by these afflictions when they happened. They would remember that the Lord had predicted persecution; they would know that it was all a part of His plan for their lives. The Lord had not told them much about this earlier because He was with them. There was no need to trouble them or to cause their minds to wander from the other things He had to teach them. But now that He was leaving them, He must tell them of the path that lay ahead for them.

## The Coming of the Spirit of Truth (16:5-15)

Verse 5 seems to express disappointment that the disciples were not more interested in what was ahead for the Lord. Although they had asked in a general way where He was going, they had not seemed too interested. They were more concerned with their own future than with His. Before Him lay the cross and the grave. Before them lay persecution in their service for Christ. They were filled with sorrow over their own troubles rather than over His. However, they would not be left without help and comfort. Verse 7 contains the promise of the Holy Spirit. Christ would send the Holy Spirit to be their Helper. It was expedient for the disciples that the Comforter should come. He would empower them, give them courage, teach them, and make Christ more real to them than He had ever been before. The Comforter would not come until the Lord Jesus went back to heaven and was glorified. Of course, the Holy Spirit had been in the world before this, but He was coming in a new way—to convict the world and to minister to the redeemed.

The Holy Spirit would convict the world of sin, of righteousness, and of judgment (16:8). This is generally taken to mean that He creates an inward awareness of these things in the life of the individual sinner. While this is true, it is not exactly the teaching in this portion. The Holy Spirit condemns the world by the very fact that He is here. He should not be here. The Lord Jesus should be here, reigning over the world. But the world rejected Him, and He went back to heaven. The Holy Spirit is here in place of a rejected Christ, and thus the world's guilt is demonstrated. The Spirit convicts the world of the sin of failing to believe on Christ. He was worthy of belief. There was nothing about Him that made it impossible for men to believe on Him. But they refused. And the Holy Spirit's presence in the world is witness to their crime. The Savior claimed to be righteous, but men said He had a demon. God spoke the final word. He said, in effect, "My Son is righteous, and I will prove it by raising Him from the dead and taking Him back to heaven." The Holy Spirit witnesses to the fact that Christ was right and the world was wrong. The presence of the Holy Spirit also convicts the world of coming judgment. The fact that He is here means that the devil has already been condemned at the cross and that all who refuse the Savior will share his awful judgment in a day yet future.

In verse 12 the Lord says there were other things the Lord had to tell the disciples, but they could not take them in. This is an important principle of teaching. There must be progress in learning before advanced truths can be received. The Lord never overwhelmed His disciples with teaching. He gave it to them "line upon line, precept upon precept."

In verses 13 to 15 the Lord tells his disciples about the work of the Holy Spirit. The work which the Lord began was to be continued by the Holy Spirit. He would guide them into ALL TRUTH. There is a sense in which "all truth" was committed to the apostles in their lifetime. They, in turn, committed it to writing, and we have it today in our New Testament. This, added to the Old Testament, completed God's written revelation to man. But it is, of course, true in all ages that the Spirit guides God's people into all the truth. He does it through the Scriptures. "He will not speak on His own authority," said Jesus. This does not mean that He would not speak *about*
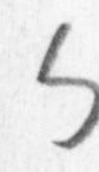
Himself, but that He would not speak *from* Himself, i.e., of His own authority. He would only speak the things given to Him to say by the Father and the Son. "He will tell you things to come." This, of course, is done in the New Testament, and particularly in the book of Revelation where the future is unveiled. His principle work is to glorify Christ. By this we can test all

teaching and preaching. If it has the effect of magnifying the Savior, then it is of the Holy Spirit. "He will take of mine" means "He shall receive of the great truths that concern me." These are the things He reveals to believers. The subject can never be exhausted. All the attributes of the Father belong to the Son as well. It is these perfections that the Lord Jesus was speaking of in verse 14. The Spirit unveils to the believer's heart the glorious perfections, ministries, offices, graces and fullness of the Lord Jesus Christ.

## Sorrow Turned to Joy (16:16-22)

The meaning of verse 16 is not at all clear. It may mean that the Lord would be away from them for three days, and then He would reappear to them after His resurrection. It may mean He would go back to His Father in heaven, and then after "a little while" (the present age), come back to them (His second coming). Or it may mean that for a little while they would not see Him with their physical eyes, but after the Holy Spirit was given on the day of Pentecost, they would perceive Him by faith in a way they had never seen Him before. The words "because I go to the Father" should not be included in this verse because they are not found in the best manuscripts.

The disciples were confused. The reason for the confusion was that in verse 10 He had said, "I go to My Father, and you see Me no more." Now He said, "A little while, and you will not see Me; and again, a little while, and you will see Me." They could not reconcile these statements. They quoted His words in verse 16, then they referred to what He had said in verse 10, "Because I go to the Father." In verse 18 they asked each other the meaning of the words "a little while." We have the same problem. We do not know whether the expression refers to the three days before His resurrection, the forty days before Pentecost, or the more than 1900 years prior to His coming again!

The Lord Jesus, being God, was able to read their thoughts. By His questions, He revealed His full knowledge of their perplexity (16:19). He did not answer their problem directly but gave further information concerning the "little while." For the world, it would be a time of great rejoicing because they would have succeeded in crucifying the Lord Jesus. For the disciples, it would mean weeping and lamentation. But it would only be for a short while. Their sorrow would be turned into joy, and it was—first by the resurrection, and secondly by the coming of the Spirit. Then, for all disciples of all ages, sorrow will be turned to rejoicing when the Lord Jesus comes back again. Nothing is more remarkable than the speed with which a mother forgets the birth pains after her child is born. So it would be with the disciples. The sorrow connected with the absence of their Lord would be quickly forgotten when they saw Him again. Again we must express ignorance as to the time indicated by the Lord's words, "I will see you again," in verse 22. Does this refer to His resurrection, His sending of the Spirit at Pentecost, or His second advent? In all three cases, the result is rejoicing, and a joy that abides.

## Prayer to the Father in Jesus' Name (16:23-28)

Up to now, the disciples had come to the Lord with all their questions and requests. In that day (the age ushered in by the descent of the Spirit at Pentecost) He would no longer be with them in bodily presence, so they would no longer be asking questions. But that did not mean they would have no one to whom to go. It would be their privilege to pray to God the Father. He would grant their requests for Jesus' sake. The words "in my name" should follow "he will give it you." Thus the latter half of verse 23 should read: "Whatever you shall ask the Father, he will give it you in my name." Requests will be granted, not because we are worthy, but because the Lord Jesus is worthy. Prior to this, the disciples had never prayed to God the Father in the Lord's Name. Now they were invited to do so. Through answered prayer, their joy would be fulfilled.

In verse 25 we read that the meaning of much of the Lord's teaching was not always apparent on the surface. He used parables and proverbs. Even in this chapter we cannot always be sure of the precise meaning. With the coming of the Holy Spirit, the teaching concerning the Father became more plain. In the book of Acts and in the Epistles, truth is no longer revealed through parables but through direct statements.

In the age of the Holy Spirit, in which we now live, our privilege is to pray to the Father in the Name of the Lord Jesus. "I do not say to you that I shall pray the Father for you," said Jesus in verse 26. The Father does not need to be urged to answer our prayers. The Lord will not have to entreat Him. At the same time, however, the Lord Jesus is the Mediator between God and man, and He intercedes on behalf of His people before the throne of God.

The Father loved the disciples because they had received Christ and loved Him and believed in His deity. This is the reason why the Lord did not have to beseech the Father. With the coming of the Holy Spirit, the disciples would enjoy a new sense of intimacy with the Father. They would be able to approach Him with confidence, and all because they had loved His Son.

In verse 28 the Lord repeats His claim to equality with God the Father. He did not say "I came forth from God" as if He were just a Prophet sent by God. But, "I came forth from the Father." This means He is the eternal Son of the eternal Father, equal with God the Father. He came into the world as One who had lived elsewhere before His coming. At His ascension, He left the world and returned to His Father. This is a brief biographical account of the Lord of glory.

## Tribulation . . . and Peace (16:29-33)

The disciples thought that they were now able to understand Him for the first time. He was no longer speaking in proverbs, they said. They thought they now entered into the mystery of His Person. They believed that He had all-knowledge and that He came forth from *God.* But He had said that He came forth from the *Father.* Did they understand the meaning of this? Did they understand that Jesus was one of the Persons of the Godhead? In verse 31 the Lord suggested that their belief was still imperfect. He knew they loved Him and trusted Him, but did they really know that He was God manifest in the flesh? In a short while He would be arrested, tried, and crucified. The disciples would all forsake Him and flee. But He would not be deserted because the Father would be with Him. It was this union with God the Father that they did not understand. This was the thing that would support Him when they had all escaped for their lives.

We find out from verse 33 that the purpose of this discourse with the disciples was that they might have peace. When they found themselves hated, pursued, persecuted, falsely condemned, and even tortured, they could have peace *in Him.* He overcame the world at the Cross of Calvary. In spite of their tribulations, they could rest assured that they were on the winning side. Also, with the coming of the Holy Spirit, they would have new powers of endurance and new courage to face the foe.

## The Lord's Prayer (John 17)

We come now to what is known as the High-Priestly prayer of the Lord Jesus. In this prayer, He made intercession for His own. It is a picture of

His present ministry in heaven where He prays for His people. As Marcus Rainsford puts it, "The whole prayer is a beautiful illustration of our blessed Lord's intercession at the right hand of God. Not a word against His people; no reference to their failings, or their shortcomings; no allusion to what they had done; none to what they were about to do as a body—'They all forsook Him and fled.' No. He speaks of them only as they were in the Father's purpose, as in association with Himself, and as the recipients of the fullness He came down from heaven to bestow upon them.

"Observe that all the Lord's particular petitions for His people relate to spiritual things; all have reference to heavenly blessings. The Lord does not ask riches for them, or honours, or worldly influence, or great preferments, but He does most earnestly pray that they may be kept from evil, separated from the world, qualified for duty, and brought home safely to heaven. Soul prosperity is the best prosperity: it is the index of true prosperity."

## Jesus Prays Concerning His Work (17:1-5)

The hour had come. Many times His enemies had been unable to take Him because His hour had not come. But now the time had arrived for the Lord to be put to death. "Glorify Your Son," Jesus prayed. He was looking ahead to His death on the cross. Were He to remain in the grave, the world would know He was just another man. But if God glorified Him by raising Him from the dead, that would be proof He was God's Son and the world's Savior. God answered this request.

"That Your Son also may glorify You," the Lord continued. The meaning of this is explained in the verses two and three. The Lord Jesus glorifies the Father by giving eternal life to those who believe on Him. It brings great glory to God when ungodly men and women are converted and manifest the life of the Lord Jesus on this earth. As a result of His work of redemption, God has given His Son authority over all mankind. This authority entitles Him to give eternal life to those whom the Father has given to Him. Before the foundation of the world, God marked out certain ones as belonging to Christ. Remember though that God offers salvation to anyone who will receive Jesus Christ. There is no one who cannot be saved by trusting the Savior. Eternal life is obtained by knowing God and the Lord Jesus Christ. The only true God is in contrast to idols, which are not genuine gods at all. The name of Jesus Christ is mentioned together with God the Father's as being the joint source of eternal life and means that They are equal. Notice that the Lord spoke of Himself as being Jesus Christ. The word "Christ" is the same as "Messiah." Jesus claimed to be the Messiah.

When the Lord uttered the words in verse 4, "I have glorified You on the earth: I have finished the work which You have given Me to do," He was speaking as if He had already died, been buried, and risen again. He had glorified the Father by His sinless life, by His miracles, by His suffering and death, and by His resurrection. He had finished the work of salvation the Father had given Him to do. As someone as said, "The crucifixion brought glory to the Father. It glorified His wisdom, faithfulness, holiness, and love. It showed Him wise, in providing a plan whereby He could be just, and yet the justifier of the ungodly.—It showed Him faithful in keeping His promise, that the seed of the woman should bruise the serpent's head.—It showed Him holy, in requiring His law's demands to be satisfied by our great Substitute.—It showed Him loving, in providing such a Mediator, such a Redeemer, and such a Friend for sinful man as His co-eternal Son.

"The crucifixion brought glory to the Son. It glorified His compassion, His patience, and His power. It showed Him most compassionate, in dying for us, suffering in our stead, allowing Himself to be counted sin and a curse for us, and buying our redemption with the price of His own blood.—It showed Him most patient, in not dying the common death of most men, but in willingly submitting to such pains and unknown agonies as no mind can conceive, when with a word He could have summoned His Father's angels, and been set free.—It showed Him most powerful, in bearing the weight of all transgressions of the world, and vanquishing Satan, and despoiling him of his prey."

Before Christ came into the world, He dwelt in heaven with the Father (17:5). When the angels looked upon the Lord, they saw all the glory of Deity. To every eye, He was obviously God. But when He came among men, the glory of Deity was veiled. Though He was still God, it was not apparent to most onlookers. They saw Him merely as the carpenter's Son. Here the Savior is praying that the visible manifestation of His glory in heaven might be restored. The words "glorify Me together with Yourself" mean "glorify Me with Your presence in heaven. Let the original glory which I shared with Thee before My incarnation be resumed." This clearly teaches the pre-existence of Christ.

## Christ Prays for His Disciples (17:6-19)

Jesus had manifested the Father's Name to the disciples. The "Name" in Scripture stands for the Person, His attributes, and character. Christ had fully declared the Father (17:6). The disciples had been given to the Son out of the world. They were separated from the unbelieving mass of mankind and set apart to belong to Christ. "They have kept Your word," said the Lord. In spite of all their failures and shortcomings, He credits them with having believed and obeyed His teaching. "Not a word against His people, no allusion to what they had done or were about to do—forsake Him."

The Savior had perfectly represented His Father, He had explained to the disciples that He did not speak or act by His own authority, but only as the Father instructed Him. So they knew that the Father had sent the Son. Moreover Christ did not originate His own mission. He came in obedience to the Father's will. He was the perfect Servant of Jehovah.

As High Priest, He prayed for the disciples, not for the world. Of course Christ did pray for the world. On the cross, He prayed, "Father, forgive them; for they know not what they do." But here inverse 9 He was praying as the One who represents believers before the throne of God. There His prayer can only be for His own.

The perfect union between the Father and the Son is shown in verse 10. No mere man could truthfully say these words. We might be able to say to God, "All mine are yours," but we could not say, "All yours are mine." It is because the Son is equal with the Father that He could say it. In this whole section He presents His poor and backward flock, and, arraying each member in a robe of many colors, declares, "I am glorified in them."

In verse 11, again the Lord Jesus anticipated His return to heaven. He prayed as if He had already gone. His request for His people was that they might be kept by the Father as a united people. He realized they would be subjected to terrible temptations and persecutions. There would be the danger of their being divided and driven apart. So Jesus prayed that "they may be one, as we are." He wanted them to enjoy the same unity in fellowship that existed between the Father and Himself. Notice the title "Holy Father." "Holy" spoke of One who was infinitely high. "Father" spoke of One who was intimately nigh.

While He was with the disciples, the Savior kept them in the Father's Name (that is, by His power and authority) and true to Him. "None of them is lost," said Jesus, "but the son of perdition." *The son of perdition* was

Judas. This does not mean that Judas was one of those given to the Son by the Father, that Judas was once a genuine believer. It means this—"Those whom You gave Me I have kept, and none of them is lost, except the son of perdition, that the scripture might be fulfilled." The title "the son of perdition" means Judas was destined to eternal damnation. Judas was not compelled to betray Christ in order to fulfill prophecy, but he chose to betray the Savior and in so doing fulfilled Scripture.

The Lord now explained, in verse 13, why He was praying in the presence of His disciples. It was as if He said to them: "These are intercessions which I shall never cease to make in heaven before God; but I make them now in the world, in your hearing, that you may more distinctly understand how I am to be employed there in promoting your welfare, so that you may be made in large measure partakers of My happiness." The Lord gave the Word to the disciples, and they received it. As a result, the world turned on them and hated them. They had the characteristics of the Lord Jesus, and so the world hated them. They did not fit in with the world's scheme of things. The Lord does not want the Father to take believers home to heaven immediately. They must be left here to grow in grace and to witness for Christ. Christ's prayer is that they might be kept from the evil, or from the evil one. Not escape, but preservation. The Christian is not of the world, even as Christ was not of the world. He should remember this when tempted to engage in some worldly pastime or enter into worldly associations where the Name of Jesus is unwelcome.

To sanctify in verse 17 means to set apart. The Word of God has a sanctifying effect on believers. As they read it and obey it, they are set apart as vessels that are fit for the Master's use. That is exactly what the Lord Jesus was praying for here. He wanted a people who were set apart to God from the world, and usable by God. 'Thy word is truth," Jesus said. He did not say, as so many do today, "Thy word *contains* truth," but "Thy word *IS* truth."

The Father sent the Lord Jesus into the world to reveal the character of God to men (17:18). As the Lord prayed, He realized that He would soon be going back to heaven. But future generations would still need some witnesses concerning God. This work must be done by believers, through the power of the Holy Spirit. Christians can never represent God as perfectly as the Lord Jesus did because they can never be equal with God. But believers are here just the same to represent God to the world. It is for this reason the Lord Jesus sent them into the world.

To sanctify does not necessarily mean to make holy. The Lord *is* holy as to His personal character. Yet here He says, "I sanctify myself." The thought is that the Lord *set Himself apart* for the work His Father sent Him to do. The thought may also be that He set Himself apart by taking His place outside the world and entering into the glory. "His sanctification is the pattern of, and the power for, ours," says Vine. We should be set apart from the world and find our portion with Him.

## Christ Prays for All Believers (17:20-26)

From verse 20 on the High Priest now extended His prayer beyond the disciples. He prayed for generations yet unborn. In fact, everyone who is a believer can say, as he reads this verse, "Jesus prayed for me." The prayer was for unity among believers, but this time it was with the salvation of sinners in view (17:21). Between the Father and the Son, there is unity of life and purpose. Believers have the life of Christ and should thus act in harmony with the Lord and with one another. This verse does not teach that the entire world will believe. But Christians, by a united testimony, should present a strong inducement for belief. When Christ comes back with His saints, and this unity is visibly displayed, the world will then know that the Father sent the Lord Jesus. But we should be seeking to reveal this truth in the meantime.

In verse 11, the Lord prayed for unity in fellowship. In verse 21, He prayed for unity in witness-bearing. Now in verse 22 He prays for unity in glory. This looks forward to the time when saints will receive their glorified bodies. "The glory which You gave me" is the glory of resurrection and ascension.

We do not have this glory yet. It has been given to us as far as the purposes of God are concerned, but we will not receive it until the Savior takes us to heaven. It will be manifested to the world when Christ returns to set up His kingdom on earth. At that time, the world will realize the vital unity between the Father and the Son, and the Son and His people, and will believe (too late) that Jesus was the Sent One from God. The world will not only realize that Jesus was God the Son, but it will also know that believers were loved by God just as Christ was loved by God. That we should be so loved seems almost incredible, but there it is!

What a great promise we see in verse 24. The Son desires to have His people with Himself in glory. Every time a believer dies, this prayer is answered. If we realize this, it will comfort us in our sorrow. To die is to go to be with Christ and to behold His glory. This glory is not only the glory of Deity which He had with God before the world began. It is also the glory He acquired as Savior and Redeemer. The glory is a proof that God loved Christ before the foundation of the world.

The world failed to see God as revealed in Jesus (17:25). But a few disciples did, and they believed that God had sent Jesus. On the eve of His crucifixion, there were only a few of all mankind who really knew Him—and even those were about to forsake Him!

The Lord Jesus had declared the Father's Name to His disciples when He was with them. In other words, He had revealed the Father to them. His words and works were the words and works of the Father. They saw in Christ a perfect expression of the Father. The Lord Jesus has continued to declare the Father's Name through the ministry of the Holy Spirit. Ever since Pentecost, the Spirit has been teaching believers about God the Father. Especially through the Word of God, we can know what God is like. When men accept the Father as He is revealed by the Lord Jesus, they become special objects of the Father's love. Since the Lord Jesus indwells all believers, the Father can look upon them and treat them as He does His only Son. Reuss remarks, "The love of God which, before the creation of the physical world, had its adequate object in the Person of the Son, finds it, since the creation of the new spiritual world, in all those who are united with the Son." And Godet adds, "What God desired in sending His Son here on earth was precisely that He might form for Himself in the midst of humanity a family of children like Him."

It is because the Lord Jesus is in the believer that God can love him as He loves Christ.

"Dear, so very dear to God
I could not dearer be;
The love wherewith He loves His Son,
Such is His love for me."

CHAPTER

# 11

# On to Calvary (John 18–19)

## Judas Betrays the Lord Jesus (18:1-11)

The words of chapters 13–17 were spoken in Jerusalem. Now the Lord left the city and walked eastward toward the Mount of Olives. He crossed the brook Kidron and came to the Garden of Gethsemane, which was on the western slope of the Mount of Olives. Judas knew that the Lord spent a great deal of time praying in the garden (18:2). He knew that the most likely place to find the Lord was in the place of prayer. With a band of men and officers from the chief priests and Pharisees, Judas came to Gethsemane. The band of men was probably a group of Roman soldiers; the officers were Jewish officials, representing the chief priests and Pharisees. They came with lanterns and torches and weapons. "They came to seek the Light of the world with lanterns."

In verse 4, the Lord went forth to meet them, without waiting for them to find Him. This demonstrated His willingness to go to the cross. The soldiers could have left their weapons at home; the Savior would not resist. "Whom are you seeking?" He asked. The question was to draw forth from their own lips the nature of their mission. In verse 5 we see some titles of the Lord. They sought Jesus of Nazareth, little realizing that He was their Creator and their Sustainer—the best Friend they ever had. Jesus said, "I am." (The "he" is not found in the original.) He was Jesus of Nazareth. He was Jehovah as well. I AM is one of the Names of Jehovah in the Old

Testament. Did this cause Judas to wonder afresh, as he stood with the others in the crowd? For a brief moment, Jesus revealed Himself to them as the I AM, the Almighty God. The revelation was so overpowering that they were driven back and fell to the ground. Again the Lord asked them whom they sought. And the answer was the same, despite the effect which two words of Christ had just had upon them. Once more Jesus told them that He was the One they sought and that He was Jehovah. "I have told you that I AM," He said. Since it was Him they sought they should let the disciples go away. It is wonderful to see His unselfish interest in others at a time when His own life was in peril. Thus, too, the words of John 17:12 were fulfilled.

Peter thought the time had come to save his Master from the crowd by violence (18:10). He drew his sword and struck the servant of the high priest. Undoubtedly he intended to kill him, but the sword was deflected, so that it only cut off the servant's right ear. Jesus rebuked the ill-advised zeal of Peter. The cup of suffering and death had been given to Him by His Father, and He intended to drink it. Luke tells us how the Lord touched and healed the ear of Malchus at this point.

## The Arrest of the Savior (18:12-14)

Now for the first time wicked men are able to lay hold of the Lord Jesus and bind Him. He was taken away to Annas. Annas had previously been high priest. It is not clear why Jesus should have been brought to him first, rather than to Caiaphas, his son-in-law, who was now high priest. What is important is that Jesus was first put on trial before the Jews in an attempt to prove Him guilty of blasphemy and heresy. That was what we might call a *religious* trial. Later He was taken to be tried before the Roman authorities in an attempt to prove He was an enemy of Caesar. That was the *civil* trial. Since the Jews were under Roman rule, they had to work through the Roman courts. They could not carry out the death penalty. That had to be done by Pilate.

John explained that the high priest was the same Caiaphas who had prophesied that one man should die for the nation (John 11:50). He was now about to have part in the fulfillment of the prophecy. "This was the man who was the accredited guardian of the nation's soul. He had been set apart to be the supreme interpreter and representative of the Most High. To him was committed the glorious privilege of entering once every year into the holy of holies. Yet this was the man who condemned the Son of God. History provides no more startling illustration of the truth that the best religious opportunities in the world and the most promising environment will not guarantee a man's salvation or of themselves ennoble his soul. 'Then I saw,' says John Bunyan, closing his book, 'that there was a way to hell, even from the gates of heaven.' "

## Peter Denies His Lord (18:15-18)

Most Bible scholars believe that "the other disciple" mentioned here in verse 15 was John, but that humility prevented him from mentioning his own name, especially in view of Peter's shameful failure. We are not told how John had become so well acquainted with the high priest, but it was that which gained him admittance to the palace or court. Peter was not able to get in until John went out and spoke to the woman doorkeeper. Looking back, we wonder if it was a kindness for John to use his influence in this way.

Peter's first denial of the Lord was not before a soldier, but before a woman. He denied that he was a disciple of Jesus. Peter now mingled with the enemies of his Lord and tried to conceal his identity. Like many another disciple, he warmed himself at this world's fire.

## The Religious Trial (18:19-24)

It is not clear whether the high priest in verse 19 is Annas or Caiaphas. If it was Annas, as seems most likely, he was probably called high priest out of courtesy because he once held this office. The high priest asked Jesus concerning His disciples and His teachings. They had no real case against the Lord and were trying to make one up. The Lord answered in verse 20 that His ministry had been public. He had nothing to hide. He had taught in the presence of the Jews in synagogues and in the temple. There was no secrecy. He challenged His judges to bring forward Jews who had listened to Him. Let them bring charges against Him. If He had done or said something wrong, let the witness be brought. The reply irritated the Jews. It left them without a case. So they resorted to abuse. One of the officers slapped Jesus for speaking to the high priest in such a manner. With perfect poise and logic, the Savior showed the unfairness of their position. They could not accuse Him of speaking evil; yet they smote Him for telling the truth.

Verse 24 should read: "Annas therefore sent Him bound unto Caiaphas the high priest." In other words, the preceding trial was before Annas. The trial before Caiaphas is not described in John's Gospel. It took place between verses 24 and 28 of this chapter.

## Peter's Second and Third Denials (18:25-27)

The narrative now turns back to Peter. In the cold of the early morning hours, he warmed himself by the fire. Doubtless his clothing and his accent indicated that he was a Galilean fisherman. The man standing with him asked if he was a disciple of this Jesus. He denied the Lord again. Now it was a relative of Malchus who spoke to Peter. He had seen Peter cut off his relative's ear. "Didn't I see you in the garden with this Jesus?" he said. For the third time, Peter denied the Lord. Immediately, he heard the crowing of a rooster and was reminded of the words of the Lord, "The cock shall not crow, till you have denied me three times." We know from the other Gospels that Peter went out at this point and wept bitterly.

## The Civil Trial before Pilate (18:28-40)

The religious trial was ended, and the civil trial is now about to begin. The scene is the hall of judgment or the palace of the governor. The Jews did not want to go into the palace of a Gentile. They felt that they would be defiled and would thus be prevented from eating the Passover. It did not bother them that they were plotting the death of the Son of God. It was a tragedy with them to enter a Gentile house, but murder was a mere trifle. Augustine remarks, "O impious blindness! They would be defiled, forsooth, by a dwelling which was another's, and not be defiled by a crime which was their own. They feared to be defiled by the praetorium of an alien judge, and feared not to be defiled by the blood of an innocent brother." Bishop Hall remarks, "Woe unto you priests, scribes, elders, hypocrites! Can there be any roof so unclean as that of your own breasts? Not Pilate's walls, but your own hearts, are impure. Is murder your errand, and do you stop at a local infection? God shall smite you, ye whited walls! Do you long to be stained with blood—with the blood of God? And do ye fear to be defiled with the touch of Pilate's pavement? Doth so small a gnat stick in your throats, while ye swallow such a camel of flagitious wickedness? Go out of Jerusalem, ye false disbelievers, if ye would not be unclean! Pilate hath more cause to fear, lest his walls should be defiled with the presence of such prodigious monsters of iniquity." Poole remarks, "Nothing is more common than for persons overzealous about rituals to be remiss about morals." The expression, "But that they might eat the Passover," probably means the feast which followed the Passover. The Passover itself had been held on the previous night.

We see in verse 29 that Pilate, the Roman Governor, yielded to the religious scruples of the Jews by going out to where they were. He began the trial by asking them to state the charge against the Prisoner. Their answer was bold and rude. They said, in effect, that they had already tried the case and found Him guilty. All they wanted Pilate to do was to pronounce the sentence. We see in verse 31 Pilate trying to evade responsibility and throw it back on the Jews. If they had already tried Jesus and found Him guilty, then why did they not sentence Him according to their law? The Jews said, in reply, "We are not an independent nation. We have been taken over by the Roman power. Civil government has been taken from our hands, and we no longer have the authority to put a person to death." They thus confessed their bondage and subjection to a Gentile power. Moreover they wanted to shift the odium of Christ's death to Pilate.

Verse 32 may have two different meanings. (1) In Matthew 20:19, Jesus had predicted that He would be delivered up to the Gentiles to be killed. The Jews were fulfilling His word. (2) In many places, the Lord said He would be "lifted up" (John 3:14; 8:28; 12:32, 34). This referred to death by crucifixion. The Jews used stoning in cases of capital punishment; whereas crucifixion was the Roman method. By their refusal to carry out the death penalty, the Jews unknowingly fulfilled these two prophecies concerning the Lord. (See also Psalm 22:16.)

Pilate now took Jesus into the palace for a private interview and asked Him point blank—"Are you the King of the Jews?" Jesus answered in verse 34 in effect, "As governor, have you ever heard that I tried to overthrow Roman rule? Has it ever been reported to you that I proclaimed myself a King who would undermine Caesar's empire? Is this charge something you know by personal experience, or is it what you have just heard these Jews saying?" Pilate's reply in verse 35 was contemptuous, "Am I a Jew?" he said. He implied that he was too important to be troubled with such a local Jewish problem. But his answer was also an admission that he knew of no real charge against Jesus. He only knew what the rulers of the Jews had said. The Lord then confessed He was a King. But not the kind of King the Jews accused Him of being. And not the kind that would threaten Rome.

Christ's kingdom is not advanced by human weapons. Otherwise His disciples would have fought to prevent His capture by the Jews. Christ's kingdom is "not from hence." It is not of this world; it does not receive its power or authority from the world; its aims and objectives are not carnal.

In verse 37 Pilate next asked Him if He was indeed a King. Jesus answered, "You say rightly that I am a king." This was simply a form of saying, "Yes, what you say about me is true." But His kingdom is concerned with truth, not with swords and shields. It was to bear witness to the truth that He came into the world. The truth here means the truth about God, about Christ Himself, the Holy Spirit, man, sin, salvation, and all the other great doctrines of Christianity. Those who loved the truth heard His voice, and that is how His empire grew. Pilate asked, "What is truth?" It is difficult to say what he meant. Was he puzzled, or sarcastic, or interested? All we know is that the Truth Incarnate stood before him, and he did not recognize Him. In verse 38 Pilate hurried to the Jews with the admission that he could find no fault in Jesus.

From verse 39 we learn that it was the custom at Passover time for the Jews to request the release of some notorious Jewish prisoner from the Romans. Pilate seized upon this custom in an effort to please the Jews and at the same time set Jesus free. The plan failed. The Jews did not want Jesus; they wanted Barabbas. Barabbas was a robber!

## The Guiltless One Condemned (19:1-16)

It was most unjust for Pilate to scourge an innocent Person. Perhaps he hoped that this punishment would satisfy the Jews and that they would not demand the death of Jesus. Scourging was a Roman form of punishment. The prisoner was beaten with a whip or rod. Often the whip had pieces of metal or bone in it, and these cut deep gashes in the flesh.

The soldiers mocked Jesus' claim to be King. A crown for the King! But it was a crown of thorns. This would have been extremely painful as it was pressed onto His brow. Thorns are a symbol of the curse which sin brought to mankind. Here we have a picture of the Lord Jesus bearing the curse of our sins, so that we might go free. He wore a crown of thorns so that we might wear a crown of glory. The purple robe was also used in mockery. Purple was the color of royalty. Our sins were placed on Jesus that we might be clothed with the robe of God's righteousness. How solemn it is to think of the eternal Son of God being slapped by the hands of His creatures and of mouths which He formed being used to mock Him!

In verse 4 Pilate went out to the Jews and announced he would bring Jesus to them, but that He was innocent. Thus Pilate condemned himself by his own words. He found no fault in Christ; yet he would not let Him go. As Jesus came forth with the crown of thorns and the purple robe, Pilate announced Him as "the man." It is difficult to know whether he said this in mockery, in sympathy, or without any particular emotion. The chief priests noticing that Pilate was wavering cried out fiercely that Jesus should be crucified. It was religious men who were leaders in the death of the Savior. Often, down through the centuries, it has been church officials who have most bitterly persecuted true believers. Pilate seemed to be disgusted with them and with their unreasonable hatred of Jesus. He said, in effect: "If that is the way you feel, why don't you take Him and crucify Him? As far as I am concerned, He is innocent." He knew, however, that the Jews could not put Him to death without his consent.

In verse 7 that when the Jews saw they had failed to prove Jesus to be a threat to Caesar's government, they brought forth their religious charge. Christ claimed equality with God by saying that He was the Son of God. To the Jews, this was blasphemy and should be punished by death. The possibility of Jesus being the Son of God troubled Pilate. From verse 8 we see that He was already uneasy about the whole affair, but this made him more afraid. He took Jesus into the judgment hall, or palace, and asked Him who He was, and where He came from. Pilate is a tragic figure! He confessed that Jesus had done no wrong; yet he did not have the moral courage to let Him go because he feared the Jews.

Jesus refused to answer him. He knew Pilate was unwilling to do what he knew to be right. Pilate had sinned away his day of opportunity. He would be given no more light; he had not responded to the light he had. Pilate tried to force the Lord to answer by threatening Him. In verse 10 he reminded Jesus that, as Roman governor, he had the authority to set Him free or to crucify Him. The self-control of Jesus was remarkable. He was more calm than Pilate. He answered that whatever authority Pilate had, it was given to him by God. All governments are ordained by God, and all power, whether civil or spiritual, is from God. "The one who delivered Me to you has the greater sin," He said. This may refer to Caiaphas, the high priest, Judas, the betrayer, or to the Jewish people in general. The thought is that these Jews should have known better. They had the Scriptures which predicted the coming of the Messiah. They should have recognized Him when He came. But they rejected Him and were even now crying out for His life. This verse teaches us that there are degrees of guilt. Pilate was guilty, but Caiaphas, and Judas, and all the wicked Jews were more guilty.

We see in verse 12 that just as Pilate was making up his mind to let Jesus go, the Jews used their last and most telling argument. "If you let this Man go, you are not Caesar's friend." As if they cared for the Roman Emperor! They hated him. They would have destroyed him had they been able and freed themselves from his control. Yet they pretended to protect Caesar's empire from the threat of this Jesus who claimed to be a King! They reaped the punishment of this hypocrisy when in A.D. 70 the Romans marched into Jerusalem and destroyed the city and slaughtered its inhabitants. Pilate could not afford to have the Jews accuse him of disloyalty to Caesar, and so he weakly submitted to the mob and brought Jesus forth to an outdoor area called the Pavement.

The Passover feast had been held on the previous evening. The "preparation of the Passover" mentioned now refers to the preparation for the feast that followed it (19:14). It was "about the sixth hour." Mark says that it was the third hour (Mark 15:25). Probably Mark used the Jewish method of telling time, and John the Roman. "Behold your King!" said Pilate, almost certainly to annoy and provoke the Jews. He doubtless blamed them for trapping him so that he had to condemn Jesus. We see in verse 15 that the Jews were insistent that Jesus must be crucified. Pilate taunted them with the question, "You mean you want to crucify your own King?" Then the Jews stooped very low and said, "We have no king but Caesar." Their reply was a remarkable fulfillment of Genesis 49:10: "The scepter shall not depart from Judah . . . until Shiloh come." By their own admission, the scepter, or government, had departed from the nation. But their words also proved that Shiloh, the Rest-Giver, had come. And this was the very thing they refused to believe. "We have no king but Caesar," they cried. Faithless nation! Pilate, wanting to pacify the Jews, turned Jesus over to the soldiers to be crucified. He loved the praise of men more than the praise of God.

## The Crucifixion of the Lord Jesus (19:17-24)

The cross may have been a single piece of wood, or it may have been two cross pieces. At any rate, it was of such size that a man could carry it. Jesus carried His own cross for some distance. Then, according to the other Gospels, it was given to a man named Simon of Cyrene to carry. "The place of a skull," where Christ was crucified, may have received its name in one of two ways. It was the place where criminals were executed, and perhaps skulls and bones were often found in the area. Or perhaps the land itself may have resembled a skull, especially if it was a hill with caves in the side of it.

The Lord Jesus was nailed to the cross by His hands and feet. The cross was then lifted up and dropped into a hole in the ground. Two thieves were crucified with Him, one on the left and one on the right. This was in fulfillment of the prophecy of Isaiah 53:12: "He was numbered with the transgressors." If you have not yet trusted Him as your Lord and Savior, will you do it now, as you read this simple account of how He died for you?

It was the custom to put a title above the head of the crucified one to publicize his crime, and in verse 19 Pilate ordered that the title JESUS OF NAZARETH, THE KING OF THE JEWS be placed on the center cross. It was written in Hebrew, Greek and Latin. Alexander says, "In Hebrew, the sacred tongue of patriarchs and seers. In Greek, the musical and golden tongue which gave a soul to the objects of sense and a body to the abstractions of philosophy. In Latin, the dialect of a people originally the strongest of all the sons of men. The three languages represent the three races and their ideas—revelation, art, literature; progress, war, and jurisprudence. Wherever these three desires of the human race exist, wherever annunciation can be made in human language, wherever there is a heart to sin, a tongue to speak, an eye to read, the Cross has a message." "The place," we are told, "was high to the city." The Lord Jesus was crucified outside the city limits. The exact location is no longer known for certain. From verse 21 we learn that the chief priests did not like the wording. They wanted it to read as a *claim* made by Jesus, but not as a *FACT.* Pilate refused to change the writing. He had become impatient with the Jews and would not give in to them any more. But he should have shown this determination sooner!

At such executions, the soldiers were allowed to share among themselves the personal effects of those who died. Here in verse 23 we find them parceling out Christ's garments. Apparently there were five pieces altogether. They divided four, but there was still the coat or tunic, which was without seam and could not be cut up without making it worthless. They cast lots for this and it was handed over to the unnamed winner. Little did they know they were fulfilling a prophecy written a thousand years before (Psalm 22:18). These fulfilled prophecies remind us afresh that this Book is the inspired Word of God, and that Jesus Christ is indeed the promised Messiah.

## Jesus Commends His Mother to John (19:25-27)

Many think there are four women named in verse 25—Mary, the mother of Jesus, Mary's sister, Salome, the mother of John, Mary, the wife of Cleophas, and Mary Magdalene. In spite of His own suffering, the Lord had tender regard for others. Seeing His mother, and John, the disciple, He pointed out John as the one who would hereafter take the place of son to her. In calling His mother "Woman," the Lord showed no disrespect. But He did not call her "Mother." This surely is a lesson for those who might be tempted to exalt Mary to the place where she is adored. Jesus here instructed John to care for Mary as if she were his own mother. John obeyed and took Mary to his own home (19:27).

## The Death of the Savior (19:28-30)

Between verses 27 and 28 probably transpired the three hours of darkness—from noon to 3:00 P.M. It was during this time that He was forsaken by God as He suffered the penalty of our sins. His cry, "I thirst," indicated real, physical thirst, intensified by crucifixion. But it also reminds us that, greater than the physical thirst, was His spiritual thirst for the salvation of the souls of men. The soldiers gave Him vinegar (probably sour wine) to drink. They tied the sponge to the end of a rod with hyssop and pressed it to His lips. (Hyssop was a plant, also used at the Passover, Exodus 12:22.) This act is not to be confused with the vinegar mingled with gall, which had been offered to Him earlier (Matthew 27:34). He had refused that because it was a pain-killing drug. He must bear our sins in full consciousness.

In verse 30 we read of the great cry of the Lord. "It is finished," He cried last. The work His Father had given Him to do was done! He had poured out His soul as an offering for sin! The work of redemption and of atonement was complete! It is true He had not died as yet, but His death, burial, and ascension were as certain as if already accomplished. So the Lord announced the way was open for sinners to be saved. Thank God for the finished work of the Lord Jesus on the Cross of Calvary! "He bowed his head," we read. Some say this means He leaned His head backward.

"Not the helpless dropping of the head after death," says Vine, "but the deliberate putting of His head into a position of rest." "And gave His spirit." His death was voluntary. He determined its time. In full control of His faculties, He dismissed His spirit—an act no mere man could accomplish.

## The Savior's Side Is Pierced (19:31-37)

In verse 31 we see again how careful these religious Jews were about details even while they were murdering their Messiah. It would not be proper to allow the bodies to remain on the cross on the Sabbath day (Saturday). There would be a religious feast in the city, so they requested Pilate to have the legs of the three victims broken to hasten death. We are not told how the legs were broken. However, they must have been broken in many different places, since a single break would not bring on death. The soldiers were well experienced in such matters. They found that Jesus was dead already. There was no possibility of His being in a faint or swoon for they did not break His legs. It states clearly in verse 33 that they saw that He was dead. In verse 34 they made sure, "But one of the soldiers pierced His side with a spear, and immediately blood and water came out." Perhaps this was a final outburst of wickedness.

There is no agreement on what the significance of the blood and water might be. Some take it as an indication that Jesus died of a ruptured heart—but we have already read that His death was a voluntary act. Others think it speaks of baptism and the Lord's Supper, but this is farfetched. Blood speaks of cleansing from the guilt of sin; whereas water typifies cleansing from the defilement of sin through the Word.

Verse 35 may refer to the fact that Jesus' legs were not broken, to the piercing of Jesus' side, or to the entire crucifixion scene. "He who has seen has testified" undoubtedly refers to John, who wrote the account. Verse 36 looks back to verse 33 as a fulfillment of Exodus 12:46: "Not one of His bones shall be broken." That verse referred to the Passover lamb. God's decree was that the bones were to be maintained unbroken. Christ is the true Passover Lamb, fulfilling the type exactly. Verse 37 looks back to verse 34. Although the soldier did not realize it, his act was a fulfillment of Zechariah 12:10. This prophecy also refers to a future day when believing Jews will see the Lord coming back. "They shall look on Him whom they pierced, and they shall mourn for him, as one mourns for his only son."

## The Burial of Jesus (19:38-42)

Now begins the account of the burial of Jesus. Up to now, Joseph had been a secret believer. Fear of the Jews had kept him from confessing Christ openly. Now he boldly stepped forward to claim the Lord's body for burial. In doing this, he exposed himself to excommunication, persecution, and violence. It is only regrettable that he was not willing to take his stand for a rejected Master while Jesus was still living. Nicodemus came too. We have met him before—in chapter 3 when he came to Jesus by night and in chapter 7 when he urged that Jesus be given a fair hearing before the Sanhedrin. He now joined Joseph, bringing with him a hundred pound weight of spices. The spices were probably in powdered form and were spread on the body. Then the body was bound with linen cloth.

Almost every detail was a fulfillment of prophecy. Isaiah had predicted that men would plan to bury the Messiah with the wicked but that He would be with the rich in His death (Isaiah 53:9). A sepulcher in a garden would obviously belong to a rich man. In Matthew's Gospel, we learn that the tomb belonged to Joseph of Arimathaea. The body of Jesus was laid in the tomb. The Jews were anxious to have the body out of the way because of their feast that began at sunset. But it was all part of God's plan that the body should be in the heart of the earth for three days and three nights. In Jewish reckoning, any part of a day was counted as a day. So the fact that the Lord was in the sepulcher for a part of three days was still fulfillment of His prediction in Matthew 12:40.

CHAPTER

# 12

# THE RISEN LORD (JOHN 20–21)

## The Empty Tomb (20:1-10)

"The first day of the week" was Sunday. Mary Magdalene came to the sepulcher before dawn. It is probable that the sepulcher was a small room carved in the side of a hill or cliff. The stone was no doubt shaped like a coin—round and flat. It would fit into a groove or gutter along the front of the sepulcher and could be rolled across the door to close it. When Mary arrived, the stone had already been removed. This, incidentally, had taken place *after* Christ's resurrection, as we learn in Matthew 28. Mary immediately ran to Peter and John with the breathless announcement that someone had removed the Lord's body from the sepulcher. She did not say who had done it, but just said "they" to indicate that this was all she knew. The faithfulness and devotion of women at the crucifixion and resurrection of our Lord should be noticed. The disciples had forsaken the Lord and fled. The women stood by without regard for their personal safety. These things are not without meaning.

In verse 3, it is difficult to imagine what Peter and John were thinking as they hurried out of the city to the garden near Calvary. John was probably younger than Peter and reached the empty tomb first. It is likely there was a low opening to the tomb, requiring one to stoop to enter or to look in. John saw the linen clothes lying. Probably they were still in the general shape in which they had been wrapped around the body. In verse 5 we see that John did not enter the tomb. By now Peter had caught up and in his usual impulsive manner entered the sepulcher without hesitation. He too saw the linen clothes lying, but the body of the Savior was not there. "And the handkerchief, that had been around His head, not lying with the linen clothes, but folded together in a place by itself." Is detail added in verse 7 to show that the Lord's departure was orderly and unhurried. If someone had stolen the body, he would not have folded the napkin carefully. John followed Peter into the tomb and saw the orderly arrangement of the linen and the napkin. "He *saw* and *believed,*" that is, he comprehended. Before him were the evidences of Christ's resurrection. Up until now, the disciples had not really understood the Scriptures which stated the Messiah would rise from the dead. The Lord Himself had told them repeatedly, but they did not take it in. John was the first to understand. Peter and John returned to their lodgings, probably in Jerusalem. There was no point in waiting by the tomb; it would be better to tell the other disciples what they had found.

## Jesus Appears to Mary (20:11-18)

The first two words of verse 11 are striking—"But Mary." The other two disciples went home, *but Mary. . . .* Here again we have the love and devotion of a woman. She had been forgiven much; therefore, she loved much. She kept a lonely vigil outside the tomb, weeping because, as she thought, the body had been stolen, probably by the Lord's enemies. Then she looked inside and saw two angels, stationed where the body had lain. It is remarkable how these tremendous facts are stated quietly and without great emotion. Mary did not seem to be afraid or surprised. She answered their question as if this were quite a normal experience. She still did not realize that Jesus had risen and was alive again.

At this point, something caused her to look behind her (20:14). It was the Lord Himself, but she did not recognize Him. It was still early in the morning, and perhaps light had not yet dawned. She had been weeping continually, and obviously was greatly upset. Also, perhaps God prevented her from recognizing Jesus until the proper time came. The Lord, knowing well the answer, asked her why she wept. He wanted to hear from her own lips the reason for her woe. She supposed Him to be the gardener. The Savior may be very near to me yet not be recognized. He often comes in lowly guise and not as one of the great ones of the earth. Mary did not name the Lord. Three times she referred to Jesus as "Him." There was only one Person with whom she was concerned, and she felt it quite unnecessary to identify Him further.

Mary now heard a familiar voice calling her by name (20:16). There was no mistaking the fact—it was Jesus! She called Him "Rabboni," which means "my Great Teacher." She was still thinking of Him as the Great Teacher she had known. She did not realize that He was now more than her Teacher— He was her Lord and Savior. So the Lord must explain to her the newer and fuller way in which she would hereafter know Him. "Do not cling to Me," He said in verse 17. This does not mean that Mary must not even touch His body with her fingers. It means, "Do not hold onto Me." Mary had known Jesus as a Man in the flesh. She had seen miracles happen when He was bodily present. So she concluded that if she did not have Him physically present, then she could have no hope of blessing. The Lord had to correct her thinking. "Do not cling to Me simply as a Man in the flesh," He said. "I have not yet ascended to My Father. When I do return to heaven, the Holy Spirit will be sent down to the earth. When He comes, He will reveal Me to your heart in a way you have never known Me before. I will be nearer and dearer to you than was possible during My life here." Then He told her to go to the disciples and tell them of the new order that had been ushered in. For the first time, the Lord referred to the disciples as "my brethren." They were to know that His Father was their Father, and His God was their God. "Not till now were believers ever made 'sons' and 'heirs of God.' " The Lord did not say, "Our Father." God is His Father in a different sense than He is ours. God is the Father of the Lord Jesus from all eternity. Christ is the Son by eternal generation. The Son is equal with the Father. We are sons of God by adoption. It is a relationship that begins when we are saved and will never end. As sons of God, we are not equal with God and never shall be. Mary obeyed her commission and became "the apostle to the apostles." This great privilege was doubtless given her as a reward for her devotion to Christ.

## Jesus Appears to His Disciples (20:19-23)

In verse 19 we come to Sunday evening. The disciples were gathered together, perhaps in the upper room where they had met three nights ago. The doors were locked for fear of the Jews. Suddenly they saw Jesus standing in their midst and heard Him say "Peace." The Lord entered the room without opening the doors. His resurrection body was a real body of flesh and bones. Yet He had the power to pass through barriers and act independently of natural laws. "Peace be with you," He said. These words now have new meaning because Christ has made peace by the blood of His cross. Those who are justified by faith have peace with God. Then in verse 20 He showed them the marks of His passion, by which peace had been obtained. They saw the print of the nails and the spear wound. Joy filled their hearts. It was truly the Lord! He had done as He said; He had risen from the dead. But they are not meant to enjoy His peace selfishly. They must share it with others. So He sent them into the world, as the Father had sent Him. Christ came into the world as a poor Person; He came as a Servant; He emptied Himself; He delighted to do the Father's will; He identified Himself with man; He went about doing good; He did everything by the power of the Holy Spirit; His goal was the cross. Now He said to the disciples, "So send I you."

Verse 22 reads this way, "And when He had said this, He breathed on them, and said to them, 'Receive the Holy Spirit.'" This is one of the most difficult verses in the Gospel. The difficulty is that the Holy Spirit was not given until the day of Pentecost. How could the Lord speak these words without the event taking place immediately? Several explanations have been offered. Some suggest the Lord was making a *promise* of what they would receive on the day of Pentecost. This is hardly adequate. Some point out that what the Savior actually said was, "Receive Holy Spirit," rather than, "Receive *the* Holy Spirit." They conclude from this that the disciples did not receive *the* Holy Spirit in all His fullness at this time, but only some ministry of the Spirit, such as a greater knowledge of the truth, or power and guidance for their mission. They say that the disciples received an earnest or a foretaste of the Holy Spirit. Others state that there was a full outpouring of the Holy Spirit upon the disciples at this time. This seems unlikely in view of Luke 24:49 and Acts 1:4, 5, 8, where the coming of the Holy Spirit was still spoken of as future. It is clear from John 7:39 that the Spirit could not come in His fullness until Jesus was glorified, that is, until He had gone back to heaven.

Verse 23 is difficult too and has been the source of much controversy. One view is that Jesus actually gave His apostles (and their supposed successors) the power to forgive or to retain sins. This is in direct contradiction of the Bible teaching that only God can forgive sins (Luke 5:21). A second view is that the power promised and authority given is in connection with the preaching of the gospel, announcing on what terms sins would be forgiven, and that if these terms are not accepted, sins would be retained. A third view, and the one that we accept, is that the disciples were given the right to DECLARE sins forgiven. For example, the disciples go forth preaching the gospel. Some people repent of their sins and receive the

Lord Jesus. The disciples are authorized to tell them that their sins have been forgiven. Others refuse to repent and will not believe on Christ. The disciples tell them that they are still in their sins, and that if they die, they will perish eternally. Note also that the disciples were given special authority by the Lord in dealing with certain sins. Peter used this power in Acts 5:1-11, and it resulted in the death of Ananias and Sapphira. Paul is seen retaining the sin of an evil-doer in 1 Corinthians 5:3-5, 12, 13, and remitting that same sin in 2 Corinthians 2:4-8. In these cases, it is forgiveness from the punishment of these sins *in this life.*

## Doubt Turned to Faith (20:24-29)

"Thomas, one of the twelve, called Didymus, was not with them when Jesus came (20:24) ." We should not jump to the conclusion that Thomas should be blamed for not being present. Nothing is said to indicate why he was absent. But Thomas is to be blamed for his unbelieving attitude. He wanted visible, tangible proof of the Lord's resurrection, otherwise he would not believe. This is the attitude of many today, but it is not reasonable. We believe in many things we can neither see nor touch.

In verse 26 it is one week later and the Lord appeared to the disciples again. This time Thomas was present. Again Jesus entered the room in a miraculous way, and again He greeted them with "Peace." The Lord dealt gently and patiently with doubting Thomas. He invited him to prove the reality of His resurrection by thrusting his hand into the spear wound. In verse 28 we see that Thomas was convinced. Whether he ever did put his hand into the Lord's side, we do not know. But he knew at last that Jesus was risen and that He was both Lord and God. Notice Jesus accepted worship as God. If He were only a man, He should have refused it. But Thomas' faith was not the kind that was most pleasing to the Lord. It was belief based on sight. More blessed are those who have never seen and yet have believed.

## The Purpose of the Gospel (20:30-31)

Not all the miracles performed by Jesus are recorded in John's Gospel. The Holy Spirit selected those which would best serve His purpose. John now states his object in writing the book. It was written that the readers might believe that Jesus is the true Messiah and the Son of God. Believing, they will have eternal life through Him. Have you believed?

## Christ Appears to the Disciples in Galilee (21:1-14)

In chapter 21 the scene now changes to the Sea of Galilee. The disciples have journeyed north to their homes in Galilee. The Lord Jesus meets them there. Seven of the disciples were together at the time—Peter, Thomas, Nathanael, James and John (the two sons of Zebedee), and two whose names we do not know. Peter decided to go fishing on the lake, and the others agreed to go with him. This seemed to be a most natural decision, though many feel the trip was not in the will of God and that they went without first praying. That night they caught nothing. They were not the first fishermen to spend a night fishing without success. They illustrate the uselessness of human efforts apart from divine help, especially in the matter of fishing for souls.

In verse 4 we see Jesus waiting for them as they rowed toward the shore in the morning, although they did not recognize Him. Perhaps it was still quite dark, or perhaps they were prevented from knowing Him by God's power. "Then Jesus said to them, 'Children, have you any food?' They answered him, 'No.'" As far as they knew, He was just a stranger, walking along the shore. Yet they cast the net on the right side of the boat at His command and, behold, a great catch of fishes! So many they could not pull in the net! Jesus had perfect knowledge where the fish were in the lake. Similarly, He directs our service and there are no more empty nets. He knows where there are souls ready to be saved, and He is willing to direct us to them—if we will let Him.

John, in verse 7, is the first to recognize the Lord and promptly told Peter who at once put on his fisherman's coat and made his way to the shore. The word "naked" is often used in the Bible when a man was not wearing his outside coat. He was then *comparatively* naked, to the Jewish way of thinking. The other disciples transferred from the large fishing boat to a small rowboat and dragged the net the remaining three hundred feet to land. The Savior had their breakfast all ready—broiled fish and bread. We do not know whether the Lord caught these fish or whether He obtained them miraculously. But we do learn that He is not dependent on our poor efforts. Doubtless in heaven we shall learn that while many people were saved through preaching and personal witness, many others were saved by the Lord Himself without any human help.

The Lord, in verse 10, instructed them to pull in the net with the fish—not to cook them, but to count them. In doing so, they would be reminded that "the secret of success is to work at His command and to act with implicit obedience to His Word." There were exactly 153 fishes in the net. This number has been taken to signify the number of languages in the world at that time; the number of races or tribes in the world, toward which the gospel net would be spread out; and even the number of different kinds of fish in the Sea of Galilee. There is no doubt it speaks of the variety of those who would be saved through the preaching of the gospel—some from every tribe and nation. The fishermen knew it was remarkable that the net had not broken. This is further evidence that God's work carried on in God's way will never lack God's resources. He will see that the net does not break.

The invitation to breakfast is given in verse 12 and the disciples gather around the fire of coals to partake of the good things the Lord had provided. Peter must have had his own thoughts as he saw the fire of coals. as he reminded of the fire at which he warmed himself when he denied the Lord? The disciples felt a strange sense of awe and solemnity in the presence of the Lord. There He stood in His resurrection body. There were many questions they would like to have asked Him. But they did not dare. They knew it was the Lord—even if they felt a certain sense of mystery shrouded His Person. The Lord now served breakfast to them. And they were probably reminded of a similar occasion when He fed the five thousand with a few loaves and fishes. "This is now the third time," says John says in verse 14, "Jesus showed Himself to His disciples after He was raised from the dead." This was the third time mentioned by John. That there were other times is clear from the other Gospels. In the Gospel of John, He appeared to the disciples on the evening of the day of the resurrection, then one week later, and now by the shore of blue Galilee.

## The Interview with Peter (21:15-17)

The Lord first took care of their physical needs. Then when they were warm and had eaten, He turned to Peter and dealt with spiritual matters. Peter had publicly denied the Lord three times. Since then, he had repented and had been restored to fellowship with the Lord. In these verses, Peter's restoration is publicly acknowledged by the Lord. Two different words for love are used in these verses. We might paraphrase verse 15 as follows: "Simon, son of Jonas, do you love me more than these other disciples love me?" He said unto Him, "Yes, Lord, you know that I am a friend of yours."

Peter would no longer boast that he would never forsake the Lord, even if all the other disciples did. He had learned his lesson, "Feed my lambs," said Jesus. A very practical way of demonstrating love for Christ is by feeding the young ones in His flock. Note the conversation had changed from fishing to shepherding. The former speaks of the work of evangelism; the latter suggests teaching and pastoral care.

For the second time, the Lord asked Peter if he loved Him. But Peter replied the second time, with genuine distrust of himself, "You know that I am a friend of yours." This time the Lord told him, "Feed my sheep." There are lambs and sheep in Christ's flock, and they need the loving care of one who loves the Shepherd. As Peter had denied the Lord thrice, so he was given three opportunities to confess Him. This time, Peter appealed to the fact that Jesus was God and therefore knew all things. He said the third time, "You know that I am a friend of yours." And for the last time, he was told that he could demonstrate this by feeding Christ's sheep. In this passage, the underlying lesson is that love for Christ is the only acceptable motive for serving Him.

## Peter's Death Foretold (21:18-23)

As a young man, Peter had enjoyed great freedom of movement. He went where he wanted. But now, the Lord told him, at the end of his life, he would be arrested, bound, and carried off to execution (21:19). He would glorify God by dying as a martyr. He who had denied the Lord would be given courage to lay down his life for Him. We can glorify God in death as well as in life. Then Jesus said, "Follow me!" As He said it, He must have started to leave.

It seems from verse 20 that Peter began to follow the Lord, and then turned and saw John following too. Here John paused to identify himself as the one who leaned on Jesus' breast at the Passover supper and asked the name of the betrayer. As Peter saw John, the thought crossed his mind, "What about John? Is he going to die as a martyr too? Or will he still be alive when the Lord comes back again?" He asked the Lord concerning John's future (21:21). The Lord told Peter not to be concerned about John's end. Even if he were to survive until the second coming of Christ, this should not make any difference to Peter. Many failures in Christian service arise from disciples being more occupied with one another than with the

Lord Himself. The Lord's words were later misquoted by others. He did not say that John *would* still be alive when He came back. He only said that if such were the case, why should it affect Peter? Jesus here linked John with His second advent. John, incidentally, was the one who wrote the book of Revelation, describing the end times in great detail.

## John's Closing Witness to Christ (21:24-25)

John now added a word of personal testimony to the accuracy of the things that he had written. Then he said, "And there are also many other things that Jesus did, which if they were written one by one, I suppose that even the world itself could not contain the books that would be written. Amen," We can take this literally. Jesus is God and is therefore infinite. There is no limit to the meaning of His words or to the number of His works. While He was on earth, He was still the Upholder of all things—the sun, the moon, the stars. Who could ever describe all that is involved in keeping the universe in motion?

We have only the barest description even of His miracles on earth. In a simple act of healing, think of the nerves, muscles, blood corpuscles, and other members that He controlled. Think of His direction of germs, fishes, animal life. Think of His guidance in the affairs of men. Think of His control over the atomic structure of every bit of matter in the universe. Would the world itself contain the books to describe such infinite details? The answer is an emphatic "No."

And so we come to the end of our studies in John's Gospel. Perhaps we realize a little better why it has come to be one of the most beloved portions of the Bible. Certainly one can scarcely read it thoughtfully and prayerfully without falling in love afresh with the blessed Person whom it presents.

# Notes

# Notes

# Notes

# NOTES

# Notes

# Notes